D0106882

*Berkley titles by Steve Miller*

A SLAYING IN THE SUBURBS
*(with Andrea Billups)*

GIRL, WANTED

NOBODY'S WOMEN

# NOBODY'S WOMEN

### The Crimes and Victims of Anthony Sowell, the Cleveland Serial Killer

## STEVE MILLER

BERKLEY BOOKS, NEW YORK

**THE BERKLEY PUBLISHING GROUP**
**Published by the Penguin Group**
**Penguin Group (USA) Inc.**
**375 Hudson Street, New York, New York 10014, USA**

Penguin Group (Canada), 90 Eglinton Avenue East, Suite 700, Toronto, Ontario M4P 2Y3, Canada
(a division of Pearson Penguin Canada Inc.) • Penguin Books Ltd., 80 Strand, London WC2R 0RL,
England • Penguin Group Ireland, 25 St. Stephen's Green, Dublin 2, Ireland (a division of Penguin
Books Ltd.) • Penguin Group (Australia), 250 Camberwell Road, Camberwell, Victoria 3124, Australia
(a division of Pearson Australia Group Pty. Ltd.) • Penguin Books India Pvt. Ltd., 11 Community
Centre, Panchsheel Park, New Delhi—110 017, India • Penguin Group (NZ), 67 Apollo Drive,
Rosedale, Auckland 0632, New Zealand (a division of Pearson New Zealand Ltd.) • Penguin Books
(South Africa) (Pty.) Ltd., 24 Sturdee Avenue, Rosebank, Johannesburg 2196, South Africa

Penguin Books Ltd., Registered Offices: 80 Strand, London WC2R 0RL, England

The publisher does not have any control over and does not assume
any responsibility for author or third-party websites or their content.

NOBODY'S WOMEN

A Berkley Book / published by arrangement with the author

PUBLISHING HISTORY
Berkley premium edition / October 2012

Copyright © 2012 by Steve Miller.
The Edgar® name is a registered service mark of the Mystery Writers of America, Inc.
Cover design by Pynographx.

ISBN: 978-0-425-25051-8

BERKLEY®
Berkley Books are published by The Berkley Publishing Group,
a division of Penguin Group (USA) Inc.,
375 Hudson Street, New York, New York 10014.
BERKLEY® is a registered trademark of Penguin Group (USA) Inc.
The "B" design is a trademark of Penguin Group (USA) Inc.

PRINTED IN THE UNITED STATES OF AMERICA

10   9   8   7   6   5   4   3   2   1

Most Berkley Books are available at special quantity discounts for bulk purchases
for sales, promotions, premiums, fund-raising, or educational use.
Special books, or book excerpts, can also be created to fit specific needs.

For details, write: Special Markets, The Berkley Publishing Group,
375 Hudson Street, New York, New York 10014.

# ACKNOWLEDGMENTS

The Cleveland media did a fantastic job of covering this story, one of the biggest to land in its lap in many years. At the risk of omitting some outlets, I have to give all the props I can to the *Plain Dealer*; the Fox, ABC, NBC, and CBS affiliates; the Associated Press; Reuters; the *Call & Post*; Ohio News Network; and Alfi Scruggs at trueslant.com.

Thanks also to Shannon Jamieson Vazquez; Robert Sberna; the Cleveland Police Department; my parents, Boyd and Julie Miller; the cool folks in the Cuyahoga County District Clerk's office; Chris Fuller; and Andrea Billups.

Photographer Liz Ledford at www.lizledford.com.

# NOTABLE PEOPLE

**ANTHONY SOWELL**—convicted serial killer of eleven women

## Anthony Sowell's Family

**CLAUDIA GARRISON**—mother

**IRENE JUSTICE**—grandmother

**JA'OVVONI GARRISON**—Sowell's nephew

**TRESSA GARRISON**—half sister

**PATRICIA DAVIS**—half sister

**OWEN "UNCLE JUNIOR" DAVIS**—half brother

**THOMAS SOWELL SR.**—father

**VIRGINIA OGLETREE**—Thomas Sowell Sr.'s first wife. Mother of Anthony Sowell's half-siblings Allan, Thomas Sowell Jr.

**VELMA CLEMONS**—Thomas Sowell Sr.'s second wife

**SEGERNA (HENDERSON) SOWELL**—Thomas Sowell Sr.'s third wife

**VIRGINIA OLIVER**—Segerna Sowell's mother

**JERMAINE HENDERSON**—Segerna Sowell's nephew

TWYLA AUSTIN—high school girlfriend, mother to
   Anthony Sowell's daughter, Julie

KIM YVETTE LAWSON—ex-wife, fellow Marine

LORI FRAZIER—former live-in girlfriend, and niece of
   Cleveland Mayor Frank Jackson

## Sowell's Victims—Deceased

CRYSTAL DOZIER—last seen May 2007

TISHANA CULVER—last seen June 2008

LESHANDA LONG—last seen August 2008

MICHELLE MASON—last seen October 2008

TONIA CARMICHAEL—last seen November 2008

KIM "CANDY" Y. SMITH—last seen January 2009

AMELDA HUNTER—last seen April 2009

NANCY COBBS—last seen April 2009

TELACIA FORTSON—last seen June 2009

JANICE WEBB—last seen June 2009

DIANE TURNER—last heard from September 2009

## Sowell's Victims—Alive

MELVETTE SOCKWELL—assaulted by Sowell in July 1989

VANESSA GAY—testified that Sowell raped her in September
   2008 and that she saw a headless body in his home

GLADYS WADE—assaulted by Sowell December 2008,
   testified against him

TANJA DOSS—former friend whom Sowell turned on and
   assaulted when she visited his house in April 2009

**LATUNDRA BILLUPS**—assaulted by Sowell in September 2009

**SHAWN MORRIS**—claims she was assaulted by Sowell in October 2009

## Police Officers and Lawyers

**RICHARD BOMBIK**—Cuyahoga County Assistant District Attorney, prosecutor

**PINKEY CARR**—Cuyahoga County Assistant District Attorney, prosecutor

**RUFUS SIMS**—Sowell defense attorney

**JOHN P. PARKER**—Sowell defense attorney

**GEORGIA HUSSEIN**—Sex crimes unit, Cleveland Police Department

**LEM GRIFFIN**—Homicide Detective, Cleveland Police Department

**MELVIN SMITH**—Homicide Detective, Cleveland Police Department

**CHARLES LOCKE**—Cleveland police officer, arrested Sowell on Halloween 2009

**RONALD ROSS**—Cleveland police sergeant, tried to ID Sowell after he was arrested

**MICHAEL BAUMILLER**—Cleveland police lieutenant, investigated Sowell as part of the sex crimes unit, Cleveland Police Department

# INTRODUCTION

At the airport for my first visit to Cleveland to research this book, I got my car at Enterprise, and the fellow asked me what I was doing in town. I told him I was writing about Anthony Sowell, and he was fascinated.

"You know Jeffrey Dahmer grew up forty miles south of here," he said, trying to get some serial-killer cred. "I know people who saw the tortured animal carcasses."

At the Hampton Inn hotel downtown, the clerk asked me why I was in town. "Business or pleasure?" she asked sweetly.

I told her, and she too was intrigued. She knew every quirk of the story. "You know black serial killers are very rare," she said. "This all happened just a few miles from here. He's going to get the death penalty. He thinks he can act all crazy and get off, but no way. He was a smart guy."

Then she added, "It gave Cleveland some attention that we didn't want."

On numerous occasions when I've been talking with a group or an individual, the question of criminal motivation comes up. Most people are beside themselves when trying to get inside the head of someone who has committed tragic and savage misdeeds, seeking the ever-elusive *why?* element.

I think of the line from Noah Cross, the character in the movie *Chinatown* played impeccably by John Huston. Cross is explaining to Jake Gittes (Jack Nicholson), the private investigator, that there is a reasonable explanation for the most depraved of conduct: "You see, Mr. Gittes, most people never have to face the fact that at the right time and the right place, they're capable of *anything*."

Anthony Sowell, like wife-killer Stephen Grant in my first book, *A Slaying in the Suburbs*, and Sarah Pender, the killer in my last book, *Girl, Wanted: The Chase for Sarah Pender*, was indeed capable of anything.

Sowell's disarming, civilized speaking patterns belie a monster who killed compulsively and violently. He kept the bodies in his apartment, his basement, and his yard. The rotting corpses smelled, but he still kept them close, though he toiled with great attention to detail to keep the odors at bay, buying bags of limestone powder and wrapping the bodies in up to six layers of plastic. He actually *thought* about it deeply. Not that the stench bothered him personally—he had no problem eating McDonald's in a room just down the hall from where four dead bodies lay, with maggots and flies crawling on them. To him, the biggest problem was that the smell had the neighbors' tongues wagging.

Perhaps it is being such a slave to a compulsion that you know is wrong, that you just can't stop. Like a Nolan Ryan fastball or a Johnny Ramone barre chord—you just do what you do because you have to. It's why you live.

That's Anthony Sowell. He killed because he felt he had to.

The day I first visited Cleveland for this story was February 17, 2011, the same day another Ohio man was executed by lethal injection for murder. Frank Spisak was a triple murderer who read Bible verses in German as he lay on the gurney awaiting the injection, the last to use sodium thiopental because of its scarcity. Ohio's use of the death penalty was alive and well, and I wondered what Sowell was thinking as he heard the news of the execution. No doubt he was aware of the sentence being carried out.

Although Spisak's fate was sealed by his hatred of blacks and other minorities, and Sowell's homicidal hatred was misogynistic, both cases had elements of race. Sowell's crimes were black-on-black, but it was also being held up as a case of police who didn't care about black people. Of course, in a police department that's 80 percent black, that was a harder allegation to prove—do black police care less about black victims? Or is the entire dynamic so convoluted that it's impossible to dissect who cares less or more? Or was the real issue less about race and more about class?

And there is the opportunity factor. Dahmer could pick up kids easily because he put himself in places where his victims were. Sowell walked the streets, seeming to troll for his victims, catching them waiting at bus stops or walking down the street. And he sure knew these weren't people who would be missed. Serial killer Gary Ridgway, known as the Green River Killer, satiated himself and his need to control and kill by making sure his victims were hookers.

"I can kill a prostitute and have a lot less chance of getting caught because you don't know them, they don't know you," he explained. "The police won't look as hard as they would if it was a senator's daughter or something, you know?"

Yes, unfortunately, we do know.

To clarify some of the reporting in this book, a quote attribution that reads "says" means that I, the author, did that interview. The attribution "said" means the quote or statement was derived from other sources, including news accounts, courtroom testimony or tapes, and letters.

As always, thanks for reading.

# CHAPTER 1

*I'm too tired to kill you right now.*

**—ANTHONY SOWELL**

When Melvette Sockwell left her mother's home early on the evening of July 21, 1989, it was with a summer breeze at her back. Melvette was twenty-one years old, slight at five feet one, and pretty. She was also three months pregnant with her third child, and unwed. It was a hard road she was taking, but on that evening, her mind was free. She was finally feeling all right.

The term *finally* was relative for Melvette Sockwell, one of fourteen children born to Aretha Sockwell. Melvette's father never married Aretha and was soon gone from the scene after his daughter was born in February 1968. But shortly after Melvette's birth, Aretha married a military man, Richard Williams.

A Vietnam veteran and military lifer, Williams and the family settled in Pine Bluff, Arkansas. But once Williams retired from his twenty years in the U.S. Army, Aretha decided it was time to get out of the South.

"We're moving to Cleveland," she announced to him and the kids one day in early 1971. And that was that. The family packed up and headed north.

"We crossed that bridge, the main bridge, into Cleveland and it was like going to the carnival with all those lights," Melvette recalls. "It was lit up like a merry-go-round at the county fair."

Melvette was happy growing up in Cleveland, and she loved Williams, her first true father figure.

"He taught me to ride a bike; he was the perfect daddy, even though he was my stepfather. He taught me about how he lived in Vietnam, about the war. Back then, when my dad was in the service, enlisting was the noble thing to do," Melvette says. "I thought about it even when I was eighteen, even though the war was just over. But I didn't do it. I was already in trouble, [though] thinking now, I should have."

And Williams provided for the family. When they arrived in Cleveland, they lived in the bluff, an esteemed part of the old city that afforded a view and many roads straight down to Euclid Avenue, once known as "Millionaires Row" because of all the mansions that dotted the road. As Melvette remembers, "All the neighbors were white. It was a really good neighborhood, up on the bluff, and down the street we had a view overlooking the city."

But the area, like so many in urban centers all over America, started going to seed as the more prosperous families left for the suburbs—the so-called white-flight phenomenon—that gutted neighborhoods and left behind cheap housing and a criminal element that wasn't policed nearly enough.

Melvette started out well enough, but she too was soon living the life of the streets. As a teenager with no one watching out for her, she fell into a lifestyle of drugs, drinking, and sex. She dropped out of high school at sixteen and had one child, then another; the familiar tragedy of the city became part of her being.

Soon enough, her mother split from Williams, though Melvette continued to live with her mother and several siblings in a large, pretty colonial house on Hilton Avenue, with five bedrooms and three bathrooms. The family had enough money to be comfortable.

"I was no angel," Melvette says. "But no one can tell me I deserved what happened to me."

On that July evening in 1989, it was balmy and moist, a dewy rain falling most of the day—the kind of pleasant night that made it worth suffering through the wicked midwestern winters. Melvette walked out of her house and got behind the wheel of her boyfriend's Cadillac Eldorado, a ride she coveted. She had no driver's license, not that that ever stopped her from driving. On this evening, her boyfriend had business and so he let her take the car, and she would meet him later.

She hit some spots in East Cleveland; she had been going to bars in the area since she was fifteen. "They never

carded; we all went there, me and my girlfriends," she
says.

After the evening ended, Melvette headed over to a
motel not far from where her revelry had landed her, just
two miles from her mom's home. Her boyfriend was staying at the motel, using it as a base from which to deal
drugs. It was around 6 A.M., July 22, when she arrived.
The clubs stayed open all night if you knew the right
people, and Melvette did. But as she pulled up, she noticed
two suspicious cars in the parking lot. They looked familiar. They looked like cops.

"I didn't want to get involved with that. I was already
dating a drug dealer," she says. "I got out of the car, it
was just getting light, and I didn't know what to do."

She walked to a pay phone on Euclid, but it was out of
order.

And as if by magic, Anthony Sowell walked up to her.
It was out of the blue, almost genie-like.

"I thought later, he was probably there to buy drugs,
but I didn't know that," Melvette says. The two talked.
Sowell was a good talker. He was a month shy of thirty
years old, an ex–U.S. Marine, in good shape, talked nice,
and he calmed her down.

He said he could give her a ride home; his car was at
his house, just a block over, on Page Avenue. By now it
was 10 A.M., and the two walked together to the stucco
house, still talking. Both were drug users, although neither was holding and agreed it was too hot at the motel
to try to score. She would just go home, maybe. Or maybe

she would spend a little more time getting to know this Anthony Sowell.

Anthony Sowell was born in East Cleveland's Meridia Huron Hospital on August 19, 1959, to Thomas Sowell Sr. and Claudia Garrison. They weren't married, but it wasn't an especially uncommon thing in the neighborhood at the time. Men wandered, and women took it and bore them children if they really liked the fellows. And women loved them some Thomas Sowell Sr.

The line on Thomas Sr. went like this: he was born October 10, 1922, in Cleveland, his parents having moved the family from Athens, Alabama, a few years before. In 1942, he married Virginia Ogletree, with whom he had four children: three sons, Thomas Jr., Allan, and William, and a daughter, Janice.

Virginia and Thomas Sr. divorced in 1952, but his legend was a weighty one; word was that he was a professional safecracker and a clever kiter of checks and other financial instruments. Which is how he found himself doing prison time during much of that decade of marriage.

"When I was very young, my grandparents took us to see my dad in prison in Columbus," says Thomas Jr., who was born in 1945. "We pulled up to this big stone building and went through a big iron gate, and you could hear that big *clang* behind you. And there were these huge gun towers. And we went into a room with tables, and all the inmates came out to visit."

As his brother Allan remembered, "My father was always incarcerated when I was young."

Thomas Sr. was also a hard-drinking man, a "rolling stone, with a lotta women," Allan said, while son Thomas Jr. says he was a "philanderer." Along with Anthony Sowell, rumors of other children popped up.

And yet, Virginia would never bad-mouth her wayward, criminally inclined husband, Thomas Jr. says. Such was the charm of his father.

Thomas Sr. was in good health save for one thing; he had epilepsy, which ran in his family. He struggled with it most of his life, and he had seizures of varying severity for as long as everyone in the family could remember. The drinking didn't help, of course. But he didn't want to quit that, so he endured the seizures.

In 1958, Thomas Sr. married Velma Clemons, a union that ended when Velma died a few years later. And in 1972, Thomas Sowell married a quiet, gentle woman eighteen years his junior named Segerna Henderson.

"Thomas drank, and he would go out," said Virginia Oliver, Segerna's mother. "When men are single, you know how they are." But Segerna "was young, and she calmed him down."

The two lived around town a bit before settling into the family home at 12205 Imperial Avenue, a palatial, spacious place on Cleveland's east side that Thomas had inherited from his father.

Thomas Sowell Sr. continued to move in and out of the prison system. In August 1977, he was charged with carrying a concealed, loaded weapon, a serious offense for an ex-felon.

He pled guilty and received a sentence of one to four years. In February 1978, he again headed to the Correctional Medical and Reception Center in Columbus to await further prison designation; but by May, with the help of some good lawyering, he was released in an order from Judge Roy F. McMahon, who ordered that Thomas Sowell Sr. be "placed on probation for a term of three years on condition of good behavior, etc."

With Thomas Sowell Sr.'s legal tussles, his fondness for drink, and the prison terms, for Anthony Sowell, there was never any real fathering. His dad asked Allan to hang out with him when Sowell was seven or eight years old, but Allan was already a man of twenty-four with career concerns.

"I took him to a softball game, a couple of baseball games," Allan said. "My father asked me to spend some time with him because he wanted [Anthony] to know the family."

On that summer morning in 1989—night was over, and it was now the next day—Anthony Sowell walked alongside Melvette Sockwell, who was a little buzzed and a little distressed over the fate of her drug-dealing boyfriend.

In January 1985, Sowell had been honorably discharged from the Marines after serving two four-year hitches. He'd come home to East Cleveland, a wiry five feet eleven, 160 pounds of muscle, and moved back into the home he grew up in, on Page Avenue. His half sister Tressa Garrison lived in the house with their mother, Claudia, and many children from various fathers and with familial ties to varying generations. Some of the kids belonged to Tressa; others came from other relatives in the loosely knit Sowell-Garrison clan.

Sowell began working as a metal fitter at an auto parts shop on Euclid, a bus ride away. It was part of his release, gainful employment. But he always liked to work.

Nevertheless, the neighborhood was eroding as well as his sense of well-being. Nearly a quarter of East Cleveland lived below the poverty line, which was determined as a family of four with annual cash income of less than $10,989.

It was a place that Anthony Sowell had once thought of as his home, but it didn't feel quite that way anymore. And whatever his demons were, the unsettled life he was living was feeding them.

Sowell and Melvette walked up the slight incline on Page Avenue to 1878, at the end of the block. The four-bedroom stucco home had been built in 1907 and featured a peaked roof; a small, stone porch with an overhang; and a stoop. A detached garage was too small for a car but instead held landscaping tools and old toys.

The house was remarkable in the neighborhood for its size—it sat on a 13,000-square-foot lot—and its imposing height. Although it was listed as a two-story building, the attic, where Sowell lived, was a functional space, with a steep stairway and a triangular ceiling. At one time divided into two rooms, it was now one large space, the domain of Sowell, as he was the oldest member of the family living there. His bed took up much of the room, and a small window opened to the front, giving the space some air.

"That was a gorgeous house," said neighbor Katie Tabb, who raised her children next door.

Sowell opened the side door to the home, and Melvette paused to look at a tree next to the garage, a bent, dead-looking thing that struck her ominously. "It was black; it had black bark. I looked at it and wondered why that was. I just thought it looked strange."

Inside, the house was filled with the smell of freshly baked corn bread and the cacophony of children playing, screaming, and scrambling.

"It looked fine," Melvette says. "His sister was sleeping on the couch; the house was okay, I thought. The kids were all looking at me, and they were smiling. [Food] was cooking. He asked me to go upstairs to his room on the third floor, and I went."

She wasn't thinking sex, though Sowell seemed "nice, not a creep. We talked about, well, certain things. But it wasn't that I was going up there just to have sex."

However, as soon as they entered the room, Sowell slammed the door, and Melvette's mind-set changed in a flash. She had been picked up hitchhiking by guys who made lascivious suggestions to her, and she had fended them off. But Sowell—now this was a Frankenstein monster that she had never encountered.

"I looked at him, and he changed, his face, his look, and I thought, 'Sister, you're in trouble.'"

Sowell locked the door with a twist, dragged a large, heavy suitcase in front of the door, and within seconds brandished the largest knife Melvette had ever seen.

For the next twelve unspeakable hours Sowell raped and beat Melvette. He would undress and rape her, then tell her to put her clothes back on. After several episodes of that torture, Sowell then tied her hands behind her back with a belt, stuffed a towel in her mouth, and took a nap.

When he awoke, he choked her until she began to black out, her tiny body losing oxygen and tingling all over. She felt like her eyes would burst from the pressure, even as black spots appeared.

She cited a mantra: "'The blood of Jesus, the blood of Jesus.' I said it over and over to myself. Not aloud."

Finally, he tired of the assaults.

"You might as well say your prayers, because I'm going to kill you," Sowell told Melvette coldly, staring straight through her. "I am going to beat you, and then I am going to kill you. But I'm going to sleep first because I'm too tired to kill you right now."

He lay down next to her on the bed, and within seconds he was sound asleep, snoring peacefully.

Melvette Sockwell looked at that small window, tilted open, and thought back to her childhood—a long, long way from where she now was—and remembered her mother allowing the kids onto the roof on summer nights. Looking up at the stars, sleeping in the open air—it was a pure pleasure that now reminded her that she was once innocent.

She also realized that escape was the only way she was going to live. Sowell had beat her with his fists, cut her with the knife, and was going to kill her.

"I was certain he was going to follow through," Melvette says. It wasn't the first time that she'd been afraid for her life. She had jumped from a moving car a few months previously after accepting a ride from two men who began to threaten her.

"I'd rather die from jumping from that car than to have them do something to me," Melvette says. "And that's what I did, and my leg was all tore up."

Now, in Sowell's room, she rolled off the bed and hit the floor with a thump. She was sure that would have waken him, but he kept snoring.

"Blood of Jesus, blood of Jesus," she thought as she crept the ten feet to the window, which had a small ledge perfectly situated to help her boost herself up. Growing up in a large family had given Melvette a necessary athleticism—she was still close to the age when she had played King of the Mountain with her brothers and other boys in the neighborhood—and even bound as she was, with her hands behind her back, she could lift herself to the ledge. With her head, she raised the single pane of glass that was the window, opening it to eighteen inches, just enough to slip her small, ninety-five-pound frame through.

That maneuver, too, made noise, but Sowell continued his slumber.

And now, she was free, on the roof in the evening darkness, beckoning to two older women on the sidewalk in front of the house.

"They thought I was playing, and they waved at first," Melvette says. "I was young looking, and they thought I was one of the kids there. I'm sure these kids were always playing. But I turned around and showed them my hands were bound; he had tied them with a necktie. I didn't want to scream. They saw that I was tied up, and I heard one of them say, 'Oh my God, call the police.'"

Within minutes, police, fire trucks, and an ambulance arrived, sirens blazing, and Melvette, lying prone on the roof, felt burly hands under her tied arms.

Melvette could not speak; the sheer terror and brutality that Sowell had inflicted on her had convinced her that a scream would surely end her life right then and there.

Two police officers joined the throng of people in Sowell's bedroom, where he, amazingly, still slept. Melvette was being tended to in the hallway.

"I was brought back into the room and saw him as he woke up and looked at the police, then at me," Melvette says. "And he told them he had to explain."

As the firemen took Melvette downstairs to an ambulance, Tressa Garrison, Anthony Sowell's younger half sister, who was among the flock of relatives living at the house, beseeched her.

"Why didn't you scream?" Tressa asked Melvette as the emergency workers escorted her down the stairs.

Tressa had heard the sirens and before the units had even arrived, she was up the stairs and through the door with her key to Sowell's room. She'd known that something had to be wrong.

But she really had no idea just how wrong.


Anthony Sowell was arrested by the East Cleveland police, and Melvette was taken to Meridia Huron Hospital. He made bond and was indicted by a grand jury in the fall of 1989, but he didn't show for his court date. The registered notice of his indictment addressed to his home on Page came back, "return to sender." It would take another crime to bring him in more than seven months later.

In the early morning hours of June 24, 1990, a Sunday, a thirty-one-year-old woman, five months pregnant, told police that she went to a house on East 71st Street in Cleveland where she was drinking with Sowell. At some point, she said, he'd come up behind her and began to choke her with his arm, at the same time letting her know that "she was his bitch, and she had better learn to like it."

He pulled her upstairs and raped her orally, vaginally, and anally. She said Sowell gave her the lines she had to repeat: "Yes, sir, I like it."

Then he went to sleep. When the victim returned with the police, he was still sleeping.

The police arrested him, but the victim disappeared. It didn't matter though because a quick check of the records found the East Cleveland rape warrant for the Melvette Sockwell assault.

For the trial, the state subpoenaed Sowell's half sister Tressa Garrison; five East Cleveland cops who had been either involved in the rescue of Melvette or the interrogation of Sowell after his arrest; the doctor who treated Melvette; the medical-records librarian at Meridia Huron Hospital; and Melvette Sockwell herself, who bravely testified for the state.

Anthony Sowell claimed to the court that he was indigent, and his court-appointed lawyer bargained the charges down to attempted rape, to which Sowell pled guilty. On September 12, 1990, Judge James P. Kilbane sentenced Sowell up to fifteen years in prison.

Eight days after sentencing Sowell was taken to the Ohio Department of Rehabilitation and Correction's prison in Lorain, Ohio, where he spent nine years, and was then moved to the Chillicothe Correctional Institution.

Once in prison, Sowell was supposed to receive sex-offender counseling, and he even applied. Chillicothe offered an advanced sex-offender treatment program, one of the vaunted elements of incarceration there, but Sowell never underwent any treatment. He was never put in the program because, as explained later by a state sex-offender counselor, "He denied committing the . . . offense."

On the other hand, Roosevelt Lloyd, who shared a cell with Sowell for several years in the 1990s in the Grafton Correctional Institution, says that Sowell refused to acknowledge his crime or take the sex-offender classes in prison because he felt it would make him a target, sexual offenders being scorned even among inmates. In the hierarchy of crimes among the incarcerated, it's better to be a straight-up murderer than a rapist. Lloyd himself was serving a sentence for sexually molesting a child, a female.

Sowell did take courses to address some of his other issues through programs with uplifting and positive messages in their titles like "Living Without Violence," "Cage Your Rage," and "Positive Personal Change." He also took the 12-step Alcoholics Anonymous programs "Adult Children of Alcoholics" and "Drug Awareness Prevention."

During his time in the Ohio correctional system Sowell received two "tickets," or write-ups for misbehavior, both on minor offenses: one for malicious destruction, misuse, or alteration of property and another for "encouraging or creating a disturbance."

What he found, though, was that prison was not as bad as it could be. His time in the Marines had made him come to appreciate institutional living. He couldn't drink, didn't mess around with contraband, and actually made some friends.

Sowell was in with the general prison population and was given a job as an electrician to begin with, tapping his military training. Being employed by the Ohio Penal Industries gives inmates time to work on products—clothing, furniture—or services, like printing.

He later handled the electronic wiring for snow-removal trucks for the prison system, and even later, he would be moved to the Madison Correctional Institution to work on engine repair in its dorms and on the yard equipment. There was other work also to which he was assigned over the years. He worked for a time in the kitchen at Grafton Correctional Institution, first as part of the prep and cleanup crew, then as a cook assistant and "shovel guy," the one who doles out the food.

He finished his prison sentence in minimum security, housed in a barracks-style dormitory within a perimeter fence. This was for people who had completed their time with little fanfare or trouble.

Parole-consideration reports over the fifteen years, culled from police statements, recounted Sowell's crime in conflicting and sometimes inaccurate terms. If the system was good at keeping people occupied and treated, it was a mess in the paperwork department.

One parole report in 1991 said:

> [Sowell] lied to female victim and tricked her into coming to his house, where he threw her onto the bed, clubbed her and raped her vaginally. She got dressed and tried to leave. He would not let her and removed her clothes again and tried to rape her anally. Unable to. Victim had recent surgery and was four months pregnant. [Sowell] raped her vaginally the second time. Then tied her hands behind her back, feet w/a belt and gagged her w/a

towel. Then [Sowell] went to sleep. She finally got
free and got out.

There was no mention of the promise of death.

In 1996, Sowell was again up for parole. The report
this time assessed the crime: "The victim was at a hotel
waiting for her boyfriend. Due to police cars in the lot
[Sowell] enticed victim to his house and raped her twice
vaginally. He threatened to kill her. She escaped by climbing out a window onto the roof, where she was found
with hands tied with a tie."

But this assessment erroneously listed the crime as not
reported until the following summer. This is the trek of
inaccuracies the county justice system would take over
the years of Sowell's criminal career.

"The case came to light 8/90, when the victim was
in the county jail on an unrelated case," the 1996
report stated, clearly contradicted by court records. "Victim
also said she had been choked and attempted to dress and
escape but [Sowell] would awaken and restrain her to
the bed."

The parole records for Sowell portray a system in disorder, complete with crime statements that conflict and
reports that have the victim included in the parole hearing when she clearly was not.

"That is something I would remember," Melvette says.
"I never even knew he was being tried back when he went
to prison. The first time I ever saw him since that day was
when he was on TV for getting arrested. And I started
to cry."

*   *   *

Melvette Sockwell's life, not the greatest to begin with, would only get worse.

She was arrested in July 1990 on a charge of possession of a controlled substance, then failed to appear for her November court date. She was sentenced to six months in state prison.

In November 1994, Melvette was again arrested and charged with possession of drugs. This time she got eighteen months in prison, probated. She violated probation and was ordered to undergo mental-health counseling and drug rehab. She violated again, spent time in the county lockup, violated again, and again. Her life was a jagged dance of mental illness, drug addiction, and jail time. There were misdemeanor charges in the city of Cleveland for prostitution and disorderly conduct. She was evicted from various apartments and houses numerous times. She had eight children along the way. The judicial system was a circus of the absurd. At one point in 2002 she was declared indigent, but part of her sentence was to donate $100 to Cops and Kids, a local program that rewards kids for keeping straight.

She never worked a regular job, and over the years she was repeatedly arrested for prostitution and numerous other small-time crimes.

Although state reports claim she advocated against Sowell's release during his parole hearings, she never heard a word of it. She didn't even hear of his guilty plea.

"I knew that if he ever got out, he would do it again. And they just didn't seem to care what I thought. They took my statement, they had me ID him, and that was it. I knew he went to prison. I just went back to the streets. That was the end for me. I am not over it."

# Chapter 2

[Growing up was] like a war.

—ANTHONY SOWELL

Anthony Sowell was not a terrifying man to look at, of course. That's what makes real monsters, unlike those in movies or folklore, so scary.

Instead, Anthony Sowell was considered by his neighbors to be an all-around okay guy. He presented well, spoke with an educated air, and smiled when he did it.

"Everyone who knows Anthony knows that he is a good cook, a good plumber, and good at everything else," said Virginia Oliver, his stepgrandmother.

His mother, Claudia Garrison, was a tough lady, born in Illinois, who had four children—Anthony, Tressa, Patricia, and Owen. No man would step forward to serve as a father to any of them, and Claudia filled the roles of both parents. From the start, she did the best she could, living with little resources, moving around the city, dodging bill collectors, and pulling what little financial help she could get from a system that had made way for the urban poor. Food stamps and other social services were a booming industry in America's cities, almost tailor-made for the misfortune of the Sowell clan.

Claudia and her mother, Irene Justice, dragged Sowell and his half sister Tressa Garrison from house to house, hopping about the lower-income streets of Cleveland, from East 88th Street to East Boulevard and from Central Avenue to Parkgate Avenue. The radius never spread more than four or five miles, a confining circle of wavering hope for something to get better.

Sowell's childhood was a murky and confusing time. He went to a number of schools, with poor results. It was inner-city bedlam during a tumultuous era for urban America, and Sowell was living the life of a bedraggled child. With a working mother, he would come home from kindergarten with a key on a chain around his neck and be alone for hours.

At the same time, Claudia's daughter Patricia was having a difficult time with her life. Patricia had been born to a fifteen-year-old Claudia and an eighteen-year-old packinghouse worker who disappeared quickly after her birth.

Patricia was sickly, with almost debilitating asthma. Yet by the time she was eighteen years old, she had five children (she ultimately had seven, three boys and four girls). But, as with her mother, Claudia, no man stuck around to do more than father any of them.

"My mom was sick all the time," says Leona Davis,

one of Patricia's daughters. "She was told not to have children, but she did anyway. She loved children."

The families merged into a caravan of illegitimate children in a household run by three generations of women: Irene, Claudia, and Patricia.

"When I first met Anthony, he was a nice kid; he was sweet," Leona recalls. "He was my age; we talked, like kids do."

In this maelstrom of nieces, nephews, grandmothers, sisters, and brothers, there was a lurid undercurrent that would permeate the family for years. There was mental illness, epilepsy, and birth defects in the family tree.

And there was abuse, something that would influence Sowell's own perverted tendencies forever.

One day, when he was around seven years old, Sowell noticed that his older nephew was forcing his niece to do something she didn't want to. At his age, he didn't know what it was, and it was only later that he understood.

"He took her in her closet and—he was like having lots of—there was a lot [of] sexual activity going on there," Anthony Sowell said. "This was happening at my sister's house. And he basically, being the oldest, he was like directing everybody [to do] what you don't really want to do, but I remember how he [took her] into the closet."

And the nephew didn't stop with his little sister; Sowell claimed that the older nephew was also molesting him, although he could never prove it.

"I don't remember what it was exactly but he was [pissed] when I bit him," Sowell said. "I got tired of him messing with my thing. I never did that before, but I bit him . . . on his arm somewhere, probably right above his wrist."

In August 1969, Patricia died at the age of twenty-seven of chronic bronchitis due to asthma. The kids moved into the house on East Boulevard in the eastern part of the city, and things continued to be nasty.

The house was jammed, seven of Sowell's nieces and nephews plus his half sister Tressa, with everyone sleeping two to a room. No one even knew how exactly they were related to Claudia; Leona never knew Claudia was her grandmother. Such was the blur of adults in her world.

And Claudia was not very fond of her grandchildren.

"She liked my sister Monica, because she had lighter-colored skin," Leona remembers. "But with the rest of us, Claudia would say, 'that black so-and-so.'"

The house on East Boulevard is where the beatings began. Claudia, says Leona, hit them with everything, from belts to coat hangers. Irene had a cane that she smacked them with. Everyone had chores, and everyone was expected to execute those chores with timely precision. All of the kids were beaten, including Sowell.

The gaggle of kids and adults moved to the house on Page Avenue in 1970. It was a big house, and everyone had his or her own room. Tressa, just four years old, slept in Claudia's room. Sowell and Patricia's son Robin took the beautifully finished attic, which was divided into two rooms at that time. Such was the hierarchy; the boys got the best.

"The house was beautiful," Leona recalls. "We had to

keep it clean; we all still had our chores. We all really had fun there when we first moved."

While living on Page Avenue, Claudia would go to work every day at a dry cleaner, and Irene would clean houses when she could get the work.

"But really, they took us kids because of the extra welfare they could get for us," Leona says.

The yard was big enough for everyone to play in, and while Claudia and Irene were at work, the kids played baseball or football all day. The yard was that big. There was also a cherry tree that they all climbed. The place was a playground.

Outside of their childhood mirth, it was an isolated world they lived in, though. No one was allowed to have friends over. Birthdays were not celebrated. There was no candy or junk food allowed for the kids, although Claudia kept her own stash. If anyone stole some, there was real trouble.

And the beatings continued in such a way that "it was psycho," said Ramona, Leona's twin sister.

"It's like a war," echoed Sowell. "There's just constant yelling and screaming. . . . All day, they were yelling at the kids, they was always going off. There's a lot of war in here."

When a perceived infraction took place—and it seemed to happen almost every other day—Claudia would have the accused strip off all of his or her clothes; then she would tie the child to the banister at the foot of the stairs and beat him or her with an extension cord or something else that gave a whiplike wound. It was sadistic and ritualistic.

"Claudia would call us down at 2 A.M. and find a dirty dish; there would be a whipping for whoever she felt was responsible," Leona says.

Worse, the others would gather and watch each other get beat.

"Both my grandmother and mother would do the beating," Sowell said. "Whupped and beaten." One night as he slept, Sowell said, his mother came into his room and started whipping him with an extension cord.

As the girls got older and more developed, Sowell and Robin watched more closely. Owen, also known as Junior, or Uncle Junior, was much older but was also drawn in by the blossoming bodies of the girls.

Sowell devised a way to satiate his interest in the girls: He would steal his mother's soda or food, then blame one of the girls, just so she might be forced to undress. And his focus was increasingly on Leona.


By the time he was in junior high, Anthony Sowell would usually walk the few short blocks each day to W. H. Kirk Junior High by himself. Built in 1930, it was a fine old school, regal and stately, a redbrick three-story building set back from busy Euclid Avenue in East Cleveland. It had a white-stone-framed front entrance, and inside, the halls were wide, and the classroom doors were solid oak. To get there, Sowell walked down Page and hung a right on Euclid, past Salon D'Le Hairstylist and the Wick Lincoln car dealership and up the slight hill on which the school sat.

He was a shy and skinny boy, "quiet and never one to start a conversation," said Cavana Faithwalker, who attended Kirk with Sowell. "If you said, 'Hi,' he would say, 'Hi.' If you asked a question, he would answer it. He was friendly, sort of, in that he would smile whenever I looked in his direction."

Sowell loved school despite not being a stellar student; he got Fs in English and Bs in physical education. But he was excited about learning and loved the classroom experience. He didn't miss much school either; records show he made it to class thirty-nine of forty days his last term in sixth grade.

Sowell tried his hand at the golf team as well as swimming and diving, but he was unexceptional. He also played chess with his science teacher, Cary Seidman.

"I was really good after a while," he says.

He was also told to choose a musical instrument to play for a performance in sixth grade. Sowell selected the cello. At a concert for teachers and parents, he played a solo of "Twinkle, Twinkle, Little Star."

"I love music," Sowell said.

When he moved on to Shaw High School, he made almost the same walk every day as to Kirk. Shaw, with twelve hundred students, was also big in the tradition of old schoolhouses, a gallant solid building with long concrete sidewalks leading up to the front doors. Its colors were red and black, and its most famous alumnus was football player Tom Matte, who went on to play for the Baltimore Colts.

Sowell was no athlete, although he'd often play basketball on the city courts at nearby Forest Hill Park.

In fact, high school didn't really give him much fun. His reticent demeanor caused him problems.

His classmates ribbed him all the time about anything, particularly his awkwardness around girls.

"I remember one time on the basketball courts a group of people teasing him about girls, being a virgin, and things in general," Faithwalker said. "He tried to talk the 'bitches-and-ho's' kind of talk, but it really wasn't part of him. A cat threw the ball to him. Anthony was so mad. He caught the ball in his stomach. He took the ball and whipped it at the guy. The guy could eat Anthony for breakfast, and would have, except another guy stepped in."

Sowell acknowledged he was picked on but blamed it on his superior upbringing, claiming that the teasing was "because I was quiet and you know all to myself sometimes . . . I just wasn't used to really associating with a lot of other kids from slums."

To some in the outside world, Sowell's childhood appeared fine. He certainly didn't present himself as any kind of predator, that's for sure.

"He was the kindest child you wanted to deal with," said Katie Tabb, a neighbor on Page. "He was always very respectable."

But academic life didn't do much for him, and he quit Shaw in the fall of 1976. Add to that the fact he had no wheels, which was a certain path to datelessness.

"He was a walker, you know?" said Chip Fleshman, a high school classmate. "To have a car as a high-school kid was a big deal." Sowell the teenager was no ladies' man, either. "I never knew him to have a girlfriend."

But Sowell did meet his first real girlfriend shortly after he stopped attending Shaw. Twyla Austin was a petite and pretty girl three years his junior. She lived on "The Hill," an upscale part of East Cleveland, relatively speaking, that shared a border with the much more illustrious Cleveland Heights.

Twyla had moved to the Cleveland area from Atlantic City, New Jersey, with her mother and siblings when she was eight, in 1969. She and Sowell met when she was walking down Terrace Road, heading home from Shaw High School. Sowell was coming from the school himself, having picked up some papers he needed to complete his failure to graduate.

"And he said, 'Hi,' and that was it—we started hanging out," Twyla says. Sowell was interesting, she thought. He was boxing in the Police Athletic League at the time, and he still loved to play chess.

Their times together were sweet.

"We would go to the den, which was where Irene's room was, and watch TV," Twyla recalls. "Claudia was never there at that time; she was working two jobs—one at Republic Steel, a mill, and the other at a laundry. And there were lots of kids around, but it was a nice place. Everyone was happy most of the time."

The house was a "mini mansion," she says. It had two kitchens and an intercom.

She spent lots of time there and recalls one day looking out the doors that led to the back porch.

"They were French doors," she says. "And there were curtains on the doors, and I saw this toy kind of hanging from those curtains. But it wasn't a toy; it was a possum. I ran and got Tony, and he just put it in a basket and let it go outside. He was real gentle with it, too."

Sowell and Twyla went to movies, taking the city bus. He always had money, somehow, but she doesn't recall what kind of job he had. He was quiet, and theirs was a peaceful, unspoken communication.

"He wasn't always showing what he knew or thought," she says. "But he was a good guy. Good to me."

Sowell also never told her about his formative sexuality, which took place on Page Avenue beginning in 1972, when he was thirteen and his favorite niece, Leona, was twelve.

"It all changed with Anthony, Robin, and Junior all of a sudden," Leona says. The almost ritualistic beatings continued, with everyone watching the humiliation of their de facto siblings. Leona watched, too.

"Anthony went quickly from being very nice to me, when we first started living all together, to being always mean to me," Leona says. "He started being mean to me as soon as he started sexually assaulting me."

One day in 1972, Sowell ordered Leona to go upstairs, to his room. And after the first time she went, and he raped her, the fight was on. Almost daily, he would tell her to go upstairs. She would refuse. Once, he blackened her eye. And so it went, over and over, for years, she says.

Ramona was assaulted by Robin and Owen. So was their younger sister, Renee. It was a madhouse.

"It was happening almost every day," Leona says.

And they were terrified to tell anyone. Claudia was still beating them, one day hitting Leona in the head with a high-heeled shoe.

Pretty soon, though, the girls began to run away, preferring to escape than face the wrath of Claudia, who didn't believe anything they said anyway.

Ramona was caught the first time she ran off and put in Metzenbaum Children's Center, a temporary shelter and diagnostic center for troubled and runaway kids. Leona willingly followed her, managing to sneak into the facility and hide for two months before being detected.

The system failed them over and over, returning them to Page Avenue and their life of torment.

Finally, Leona figured a way out.

"I set some clothes on fire in Claudia's room while she was at work. It was summertime, and everyone else was downstairs. I went up there, closed the door. I had some matches, and I lit those clothes. I walked out, and pretty soon, the fire department was there because there was smoke coming out the window, and someone called them. And I confessed. I finally got into Metzenbaum myself, and I never had to go back to Page. I got admitted to Sagamore Hills Children's Psychiatric Hospital. And someone there believed me."

Still, Leona's fortunes didn't improve all that much. Her life from then on became a blur of suicide attempts, blackouts, psychotic episodes, and advanced mental illness, all a hangover of her days on Page at the hands of Anthony Sowell.

By the late 1970s, East Cleveland was falling apart, part of the urban decay sweeping America. The town of 40,000 was losing population, leaving only the poor, primarily black residents to hold down the place. To be from C-Town, as East Cleveland was called, was to be from poverty.

"It was getting to be terrible, just terrible," recalls Twyla Austin.

The stretch of once glitzy Euclid Avenue was now a decrepit haven of drug dealing and thuggery.

Anthony Sowell was also starting to find trouble; by 1977, he was a high school dropout with a varied trail of misdemeanors, including shoplifting, domestic violence, drunk and disorderly, breaking and entering, and minor assault.

He paid a fine for the disorderly charge and served thirty days on the domestic violence case. The aggravated burglary charges were dropped. The police had bigger fish to fry.

For the first time in his life, Sowell had to make a move on his own. He lacked the credits for a high school diploma. So, like quite a few of his peers, facing a life of crime or poverty, armed for life with nothing more than some minor street smarts, in the spring of 1977, Sowell enlisted in the U.S. Marine Corp (though he first tried to join the army before changing his mind).

He was underage, still only seventeen, and his mother, Claudia, didn't approve. "She argued against it, but she end[ed] up signing the papers, because this might happen anyway when I turn eighteen in August that year [1977]," Sowell said. "I finished school when I was seventeen, so I was going. I got into the Marines. That started off early that year. I actually signed up with the army—I was literally with the army at first. Early that year, around February or March [1977], I started at the recruiting camp at school but then [the army recruiter] came up, and he started talking to me and talked to my parents, and I initially took my entrance test with the United States Army."

The Marines, he said, were tougher and that's where he went "because I have a point to prove," he said. "That I can do it."

He had told Twyla that he was considering the move.

"But he never gave me any real reason, and I supported him doing it," she says. It would give him some money, and he was going to need it; a month after he left Cleveland for training, Twyla called and told him she was pregnant.

"He was really happy," Twyla says. "I think he was proud."

A daughter, Julie, was born in August 1978.

Sowell reported for boot camp on January 24, 1978, at Parris Island, South Carolina, before being dispatched for basic training at Camp Lejeune, in North Carolina.

It was the smartest thing Sowell would ever do, and his time in the Marines was marked with success, at least professionally.

He finished first in his basic-training class of forty. Soon he would find that he could hit a target with a rifle from 600 yards. Like all Marines, Anthony Sowell was taught how to defend himself and emerge victorious from battlefield conflicts, how to hurt an enemy by hand, using choke holds, punches, and weapons in hand-to-hand combat. These are special fighting skills, similar to those taught and embraced by the vaunted U.S. Navy SEALs.

In May 1978, Sowell began his military career as an electrician at Camp Lejeune, first obtaining his high school equivalency and then studying electrical wiring before moving up the coast to Cherry Point, where he stayed until March 1980 with the Second Marine Aircraft Wing, an aviation unit supporting Marine ground operations in wartime. A solid Marine, Sowell moved around a lot, adapting anywhere he went. He even boxed in the camp boxing clubs, again showing he had something to prove.

He next moved on to Camp Smedley D. Butler with the Third Force Service Support Group, Fleet Marine Force Pacific, in Okinawa, Japan, for a year.

It was there that he met Kim Yvette Lawson, an officer.

For Sowell, it was the best relationship he would ever have in his life.

"She understood me better, could handle me better than anyone I ever seen," he said. "I don't know, we just had that connection. I know I had come up from a bad— I had a bad childhood, and after we got married I had, you know, I had some issues that she helped me on.

"I could be affectionate but she was one of those really touchy kinds of females and I could just learn just one time . . . we'd be sitting on the couch and I think she put her arm around me or something like that, I [would] almost act violent. . . . I didn't like her touching me like that," he later confessed.

But Kim, he said, helped him learn to accept love.

They were married in 1981 in a civil ceremony in New Bern, North Carolina, at the Craven County Courthouse after both returned to Cherry Point

The ceremony was performed by a magistrate, and the couple moved to a trailer in a small, seven-unit trailer park located off-base in a remote area.

During that time, Sowell endured a traumatic injury while working on his car. His daughter, Julie, and his sister Tressa were visiting the couple, and Claudia was on her way as well.

"My sister and my daughter had been down to visit me and my mom was on the way to come down at night," Sowell said. "A friend of mine, another Marine, was being transferred to Washington, D.C., the next day and so he was having—him and his wife were having a going away party and because my mom was coming, Kim had to stay home plus you know my daughter and sister was there too and she—my sister was only sixteen. So my wife stayed home and I went ahead to the party. On my way home, my car overheated and shut off, and when I went up by the hood, and when—I was messing around because it was hissing at the hose—It just blew off and when it blew off, they pointed straight to my face so it did hit me in the face but I didn't have a chance to close my eyes so it actually just hit me straight to my eyes and my face."

Sowell received second- and third-degree burns, and it split his eyes. He was blind for more than three months. Kim nursed him the whole time.

"That's all I had," Sowell said. "Well, I didn't want my sister and daughter there, you know going through that, so I just sent them home."

But if Kim represented everything good to him, her mother said her daughter told her Sowell was drinking to excess. She married him to help him.

"She didn't want him to get a dishonorable discharge," said Kim's mom, Norma Lawson. "She was trying to get him through the Marine Corps."

The marriage was marked mostly by transition; both Kim and Sowell were on the move and spent only two years physically together, because in January 1984, Sowell was again transferred back to Camp Butler, in Okinawa.

The couple divorced less than a year later, shortly before Sowell left the Marine Corps, in January 1985. "She divorced him the day she got out," Norma Lawson said. Sowell later told a prison counselor that the couple split because of the physical distance their Marine careers required. Kim Lawson later died in 1998, in an industrial accident back in California, her home state.

Sowell served the last of his tour of duty at Camp Pendleton, California.

His military stint was marked by his good performance; Sowell received awards during his seven-year Marine Corps career, including a Good Conduct Medal with one star, a Meritorious Mast certificate, a Sea Service Deployment ribbon, a Certificate of Commendation, and two Letters of Appreciation.

"He did exceptionally well . . . Mr. Sowell was promoted meritoriously to private first class at the end of recruit training, which is an extreme distinction," said Walter Bansley III, a military lawyer who analyzed Sowell's military records.

Unfortunately, then he came home. And was never quite the same.

If East Cleveland was in decline when Anthony Sowell left, it was a full-on ghetto when he returned. It was plagued by crime and had a city government infused with ineptitude and corruption.

Crack, a smokable form of cocaine that many people found irresistible, was decimating inner cities all over the United States. Crack came to the cities of America in 1986, although its cousin, freebase, had been around since the early 1970s. Crack was essentially pure cocaine; the recipe was cocaine, baking soda, and water. The coke was dissolved in water and baking soda and dried.

Smoked by users in a metal chamber hollow on both ends called a stem, or a glass pipe that can be made of anything, from a piece of Pyrex to glass tubes used to sell single-stem roses, crack was characterized by its burnt-hair odor and its ability to hit the user in a flash, creating a rush; it was an orgasmic flush that went through pleasure zones that many didn't even know they had.

The drug became popular in coordination with a surplus of cocaine on the streets of America via South America. The supply drove the price down, and the intensity of a crack high drove its allure up. It was a potent piece of math. Crack was initially dubbed "Ready Rock" in Los Angeles, where it caught on first, because cocaine pieces were called rocks and it was being sold in a ready-to-smoke form.

Crack is heavily addictive because of the speed with which it reaches the brain. Although people who snort cocaine get high, it takes some time for the drug to hit the pleasure center, as it's absorbed through the nasal membranes. The lungs, however, have a ready connection to the bloodstream. The rush creates the motivation to repeat the ingestion. Over and over.

"It's like once you smoke it, it's like a big rush, and it doesn't last but five seconds," says Dawnetta Cassidy, who hung out in the Imperial neighborhood over the years. "And that's why everybody likes it. It's the drug that makes you run back and forth. You just don't get up and leave. You gotta have the next hit."

The Imperial neighborhood was riddled with the drug in 1990, when Sowell was sent to prison, but it was an epidemic by the time he was released, in 2005.

But in 1985, after his discharge from the Marines, Sowell, who loved his booze and weed, would find almost everyone he ran into smoking crack on these streets. It was an amazing change for him; the very Euclid Avenue on which he used to walk to school was now a hotbed of drug sellers. And with those vendors came women willing to do anything to obtain crack.

Anything.

And Sowell could just imagine what that meant.

He was a divorced twenty-five-year-old with a predilection for drinking, dogged by the fatherly demands for a seven-year-old daughter he had out of wedlock, and a family situation that was more like war, as he put it, than anything else. He began drinking as often as he could, which was very often. He began drinking in the morning. He had blackouts and cravings. Almost every day, there was booze, mostly beer, sometimes liquor. He moved into the attic of the house on Page Avenue, now converted from two bedrooms into one large space. He met girls, but things never worked out.

And he was angry.

"He was very direct . . . You see the change when they go into the Marines," his half sister Tressa described it later. She saw it when she stayed with her brother and his wife, Kim, in North Carolina as a teenager. He was much more serious, less lighthearted.

"They come back very different," she said. "Very stern, almost."

By the time Sowell returned to Cleveland, Twyla had moved into Tressa's house with their daughter, Julie, although Sowell made it clear they were not a couple. He took the full upstairs room for himself—"He sort of kicked me out, and I moved downstairs," Twyla says—and hid out up there.

"He just stayed up there, and rarely came out, although he would be a good father for Julie," says Twyla, who was working at a nearby restaurant. "He would come down and play with her. But other than that, he was either out or up in the room."

And he had started using drugs, she says. "He was snorting cocaine, which he had never done before," Twyla says. "He wasn't smoking crack. [But] he was drinking and snorting coke."

And the encounters with the law grew more frequent. Sowell was arrested in 1988 on a domestic-violence charge, and he served eight days in the East Cleveland jail.

He was violent with others, too. One day, a girl in the neighborhood got in Tressa's face. Sowell, drunk, didn't like it.

"He hit this girl that was talking to me 'cause she was talkin' to me real aggressively, and Sowell said one time, he was like, 'Leave her alone,' and she kept on talkin', kept on talkin'; next minute all he did was hit her once. She was bleeding all over the place," recalled Tressa.

Soon enough, Sowell began to sample crack, which agitated him even more. He got popped once for possession of cocaine, and between 1986 and 1989, he was arrested numerous times on charges, including public intoxication and disorderly conduct. East Cleveland police records, though, are in the same state for that time period as the city: complete disarray.

It was a bad time.

And it got worse.

# Chapter 3

A low probability rating to reoffend . . .

**—OHIO DEPARTMENT OF REHABILITATION AND CORRECTION**

The fifteen-year sentence served by Anthony Sowell for the assault of Melvette Sockwell was hardly an eye-opener for him. Although he had a few problems with his fellow inmates, he was slow to understand the severity of his crime.

Perhaps more telling, he seemed to thrive in prison. "I liked the institutional life," Sowell says, comparing his time in prison to his time in the Marines, though noting the difference between the military, where he went voluntarily, and prison, to which he was sentenced.

Written explicitly, baldly, on a parole department form for Anthony Sowell in the Ohio Department of Rehabilitation and Correction file in 1996: "Continue to maximum expiration of sentence." Also in the same file was the phrase "lack of significant programming," meaning Sowell was not grasping the behavioral changes he needed to embrace in order to make parole on the Sockwell charge. He was barely halfway through his time, and he hadn't figured it out.

While he was in the prison system, Sowell was given a questionnaire to fill out, the kind of thing that prison shrinks administer to evaluate inmates upon release.

I like: Nothing of what I'm going through

The happiest time: Will be when I get out of jail

Men: Are men and boys are boys

The best: Is yet to come

What annoys me: Things that are going on in the world

A mother: Is a best friend and a mom

I feel: Nothing at this time of my life

I can't: Wait to get back home

Sports: Is one of my favorite things

When I was a child: My mother gave me all a child would want

My nerves: Are just fine

Other people: Get on my nerves sometimes

I suffer: No ill feelings

I failed: To get myself out of trouble

Reading: Is best for the mind

I need: To be at home

Marriage: Was in my life at one time but now it's gone

I am best when: I'm at work

I hate: Getting sent to jail

This place: Needs to feed us more food

I am very: Special person to me

I wish: I was out of here

My father: Is the best
The only trouble: I will get in is this
I secretly: Have no secrets
Dancing: Is best done by two
My greatest worry is: Not getting out of here
Most women: Just tell lies

It was hardly encouraging.

In lockup, Sowell got along well with the other prisoners, but he had a telling quirk.

"[In prison] he wasn't that bad of a guy. It wasn't like he presented any kind of threat to anybody," said an inmate who served with Sowell at Grafton Correctional Institution. "Sowell stood out because of the way he wanted you to pronounce his name. He wanted it pronounced *So Well*." Most people typically pronounced it *Soul*.

But he didn't get mad about someone getting it wrong and delivering it in the traditional, one-syllable fashion, unless the person was a female.

"Those lady [correctional officers] was pretty much who he went off on when they pronounced his name wrong. If it was one of us, he was like, 'Man, it's *So Well*.'"

After serving his whole sentence of fifteen years, on Monday, June 20, 2005, Sowell walked out of the Lorain Correctional Institution in Grafton, Ohio.

The release was a family affair; Tressa bundled a bunch of her ever-growing brood of kids into the family car and headed to pick up her half brother.

Ja'ovvoni Garrison, then fifteen, who was born to

Tressa the year his uncle went to prison, says, "We picked him up from prison—me, my grandma, my mom, some other of us, got in our maroon station wagon and went to Lorain. We stayed in [the] car, and my mom went to go get him and help him be released."

The house on Page Avenue had been repossessed after the family failed to pay the mortgage, and they were all living in a rented house in an area known as the Slavic Village. The neighborhood had originally been settled by immigrants from Eastern Europe who had come to the United States to work in steel mills in the late 1800s.

"There were thirteen of us living in that one house," Ja'ovvoni says. "There were nine of us kids; three boys [and] three girls would share a room; then the younger brother and sister would sleep with my mom."

But despite the tight fit, when Sowell moved in, he got a room all to himself.

"Anthony was real quiet, and he was a really good cook. He was really into it; he was also into the idea that people respected him and that he didn't get into too much trouble in prison," Ja'ovvoni says of his uncle.

In one respect, having all the kids around provided Sowell some playmates; even though they were children and he was in his midforties. He loved the football video game *Madden NFL*, and would play solo or with the younger boys.

"And he was always the Browns—he loved the Browns, both in that game and in real life. Sowell loved sports."

But the time with Tressa and her kids was short. Sowell moved out within a few months, heading about four miles away to live with his stepmother, Segerna. It would be the last place he ever lived as a free man.

One of Sowell's first mandates as a free man was to register as a sex offender. In his new neighborhood, he was one of twelve in a five-mile radius. He was humiliated, relatives say, and he feared that it would hinder his ability to find a job. He filed applications with a number of temporary-employment contract services, including Paragon Culinary Staffing, which filled food-service needs around town.

Despite his fears, however, Sowell quickly landed what many a sports fan like himself would consider a plum assignment: working as a prep cook in a kitchen at Jacobs Field, home of major-league baseball's Cleveland Indians. The stadium sat on the southern edge of downtown, one subway ride and a ten-minute walk away from where he was then staying, with Tressa and her family, in Slavic Village. The stadium, with a half dozen kitchens and lounges serving food and three levels of suites, was a massive ode to pro sports indulgence.

For day games, Sowell would arrive at 6 A.M. to cut, dice, and julienne the carrots, onions, cucumbers, and tomatoes for salads and deli trays. It wasn't the actual cooking job he dreamed of, but for the time being, he figured it was a good way to get started in the work world. Despite his electrician training, Sowell harbored hopes of someday cooking in a fancy restaurant in Cleveland.

"Yeah, I was paid as a cook and it was good work,"

Sowell says. "I worked twelve hours a day, and for night games, I got there at nine or so. It's the best job I ever had. They let me stay after and watch the games, but by the time that happened, I was tired and just wanted to go home."

In August 2005, Sowell received a notice in the mail from the Cuyahoga County Court Psychiatric Clinic. As part of his sex-offender monitoring, he was required to undergo a sexual-predator evaluation.

On September 1, 2005, Sowell showed up an hour early to the county Justice Center, a little put out by the obligation. After all, he felt, he had served his complete sentence, he wasn't on parole or probation, and he was working twelve-hour days at a good job, one with community standing. The Indians, like the football Browns and the basketball Cavaliers, were religion among many Clevelanders.

Straightaway, Sowell was told that there could be some negative impacts from the evaluation. It was a public record.

"I know, I know," he said, his initial irritation dissipating. He had no choice, and over the course of the next hour and a half, Sowell talked, listened, and talked some more. In some cases, he told the truth. In others, he covered up.

He reported that his upbringing was in a single-parent home in an urban area, and he added that his home "was crowded."

He told the analyst that he had a lot of friends while growing up but added that he was bullied and teased as well. He neglected to tell of the sexual abuse he both witnessed and partook in. In fact, whether it was a case of covering up or of being completely oblivious, he told the analyst that his childhood was good.

The report also notes that Sowell claimed that "he was not exposed to violence in his home, school, or community" and that "he does not have a strong temper."

In doing background work on Sowell, the analyst later wrote in a report that "Mr. Sowell's grades [in high school] were average; he was never in special education classes nor did he receive tutoring or medicine for attention problems. His school attendance was generally good and he was never suspended or expelled."

Sowell said he'd never been suspended from school or fired from a job, and he had never received any government assistance of any kind, for any reason.

Asked about the attack on Melvette Sockwell, he claimed to have known her for about eighteen months at the time of the incident, an assertion Melvette denies and was never verified by the state.

"He stated that he paid her money to engage in consensual sex," according to the report. "He stated that he had used alcohol prior to the . . . offense but was not 'falling down drunk.' He indicated that he pled guilty to the charge because he was having difficulty mounting a 'good defense.'"

His attorney in that case—the one who Sowell implied was ineffective—was James McDonnell, who, many years later, would run for Cuyahoga County prosecutor.

"All I can tell you is that I remember nothing about representing him," McDonnell says now.

Sowell talked about his drinking and confided that he may well have a drinking problem although, because of his incarceration, he hadn't been drunk in sixteen years, since he was thirty.

Questioned about sex, Sowell simply lied. He said he learned about sex through talking with his friends at school and sex-ed classes and that his first sexual experience came at age seventeen with his high school girlfriend, who would have been Twyla Austin.

He admitted that he bought hookers while he was in the Marines and hit the occasional strip joint. He said that like most men, he had checked out pornography, some hard-core, but never had any violent sexual fantasies. In fact, he came off as a guy who caught a bad break on the rape charge.

To the nameless analyst, who would file this report for public consumption as well as for judges and lawyers and law-enforcement agents who look to these professional assessments for guidance in determining a suspect's possible guilt, Anthony Sowell seemed like a pretty okay guy. In the report, the analyst wrote that Sowell was "attentive throughout the interview. He demonstrated a full range of emotional expression. His speech was appropriate for rate, tone and volume. He was generally cooperative and polite. His thoughts were organized and logical. His responses were clear and understandable. He described his general mood as 'good.' The defendant's hazard recognition skills and social judgment were good." The analyst's report went on to say, "It is my opinion that with reasonable professional certainty that Mr. Sowell does not currently present with the following risk factors most significantly correlated with sexual offense recidivism."

The factors that the analyst indicated included age (at forty-six, Anthony Sowell was statistically less a risk to reoffend), gender of victim (a male offender typically indicates a higher risk), and, notably, failure to complete treatment (in Sowell's case, he had never *had* treatment; therefore, this factor was ignored—he could not be said to have "failed" to complete something he's never even begun). Also considered were prior sexual offenses (of which Sowell had none) and deviant sexual preferences (which he denied).

Sowell was given a low probability rating to reoffend. Years later, when the report was revealed to have been flawed, the county refused to divulge who the analyst was. But as a result of that county employee's poor judgment, Sowell was classified as a "sexually oriented offender" based on his attempted rape conviction, but not a "sexual predator," which would have placed him under more scrutiny when a sex crime was reported in the area around him.

The system was not working.

The Sowell family home at 12205 Imperial is a majestic house, built in 1917, in the once-great neighborhood of Mount Pleasant. It is three stories of finely honed woodworking and ornate metal framing, wrapping around gorgeous built-in bookcases, knickknack cabinets, and kitchen cabinets. Over the number 12205 is a metal plate embossed with the family name, Sowell, in red lettering on a black background. The 2,000 square feet is distributed evenly between the three floors, plenty of room for the four bedrooms and three full baths.

An unfinished basement, full of crawl spaces and little hidden alcoves, provides another 1,000 square feet for storage and whatever else one could fit around the massive furnace, which spreads its vents upward like a Medusa.

The home had been in the Sowell family for generations. John and Cleathor Sowell, Anthony's paternal grandparents, had passed the house on to their son Thomas in 1995. The whole family would take a turn at some kind of handiwork at 12205. It always needed something, and it was a fine enough house that it deserved the attention.

Going all the way back to the 1950s, there were grapevines in the backyard in the summer, and John Sowell would make wine. In the winter, the basement was turned into a skating rink.

"When I was staying there, it was the best place in the world," recalled Veosie Cox, who rented out the first floor of the house with her husband from John and Cleathor in 1954. "They were the owners of the house, the best people in the world."

Through the 1960s, the Mount Pleasant neighborhood was as robust as any place in America, booming with local groceries, flower shops, beauty parlors, and restaurants both small and large. The businesses served residents who were mostly Italian and Polish.

By 2000, though, the neighborhood was a sad ruin of

those robust days four decades before. The median local income was $22,452, among the lowest in the state. One in three adult residents of the area received food stamps. Crime was routine, windows were barred, and the grocery stores had become poorly stocked bodegas selling plenty of King Cobra malt liquor, lottery tickets, and Kool cigarettes, while detergent and other household items were sometimes marked up 100 percent or more.

"There was lots of activity in the neighborhood, always," said Lakeesha Pompey, who rented the second floor at 12205 Imperial with her husband and baby, beginning in 2003. But she was also seeing and hearing more fights, drug deals, and loud obscenities. There were gunshots in the middle of the night.

"It tended to be a little rough," added her husband, Brandon Pompey. "There was a house immediately adjacent to ours that was allegedly selling drugs."

Thomas Sr., Anthony's father, lived in 12205 Imperial for years with his wife, Segerna, sometimes joined by other relatives or various tenants. By the 1990s, Thomas Sr. quit drinking and had turned into quite the local handyman, helping others to do painting and other maintenance chores.

"But he still loved to talk about women," says Sam Tayeh, who owned a nearby market. "He was into those 'strawberries' is what we called them. The girls who smoked crack, and it seemed like all of them. But Thomas would come into the store and sit down with me behind the counter—we'd talk. He was a good guy."

And Thomas was nobody's sucker. In 1998, he and

Segerna filed a lawsuit against Brooks Financial Corporation alleging the financer had hoodwinked them in a $15,000 second-mortgage scheme. A local court dismissed the case, but the Eighth Appellate Court of Appeals, State of Ohio, kicked back the case on appeal, and in 2000, the Sowells were awarded $150,000, ten times their filed amount.

But on March 11, 2003, Thomas Sowell Sr. fell down dead on the floor of his bathroom at age eighty. The death certificate listed a number of maladies as the cause: heart disease, prostate cancer, and seizure disorder.

Segerna lived there on the first floor alone, with the Pompeys on the second floor, until early February 2006, when her stepson Anthony Sowell came by to ask a favor. In the months since he had been out of prison, he'd been visiting and helping out around the place. He wanted out of his sister Tressa's overcrowded house and needed a place to stay, someplace with a little privacy. He had money, he told Segerna, and he could pay rent.

It was agreed; Sowell initially moved into the back bedroom on the first floor, then soon moved on up to the empty third floor, after doing some finishing work on it. It had always been livable, but now Sowell redid the drywall, painted, and fixed up the small kitchen and bathroom. He created his own private apartment, accessible by a side door to the rear of the house. Segerna would never be bothered by his comings and goings that way. He got himself a cheap computer with some of the money from his Cleveland Indians job so he could have e-mail, although the only connection he could afford was an analog.

"I had a land phone line for my computer," Sowell says. It was slow, he said, but he used the computer at his "sister's place or the library or the programs I was in" as a former prisoner.

He didn't care. The world was new after being locked away for fifteen years. He had some time to make up for.

The Cleveland Indians job ended with the season on October 2, 2005, and Anthony Sowell got another job, at Nampak, an international packaging operation; then he landed a job as a machine operator, doing molding injection at Custom Rubber in March 2006.

It was a decrepit, greasy shop, near the lake, nestled among other decrepit, greasy industrial joints, including a metal fabricator, a printing shop, and an auto-repair shop that could well have been a chop shop. On the front of Custom Rubber was a sign that claimed it to be a "drug free workplace . . . all applicants will be tested prior to hiring." Somehow Sowell, a habitual pot smoker, apparently managed to avoid Custom Rubber's self-proclaimed stringent requirements. Inside, workers toiled under dim lights that cast a yellow pall on everyone and everything. It was the stereotype of a shop job.

But it was a union shop with solid pay, and for Sowell, it was a good place to land. Sometimes, rather than taking the bus, he would walk the six miles to work, ninety-minutes one-way on foot.

He began to become known around the Mount Pleasant neighborhood as a friendly guy, a drinker, of course, but nothing more than that, as far as anyone knew. He had a good line of patter—he could talk about the Marines, prison life, food, sports, travel, any number of manual-labor skills like plumbing or electronics. People called him Tony or Tone.

"He came in here when he first moved to 12205," says Sam Tayeh, the convenience-store owner. "He was sharp, well dressed. He was quiet, but when he got here at first, he came in and asked, 'Are you Sam?' I told him I was."

"I want to thank you for taking care of my parents," Sowell told him. "My father was Thomas Sowell, and my stepmother is Segerna. They say you were very kind to them, and I need to thank you."

It was an unusually pleasant interaction with a neighbor for Sam Tayeh. Tayeh had been born in Jerusalem and came to the United States in 1977 to join family members who owned a bodega in the Bedford-Stuyvesant neighborhood in Brooklyn. In 1992, he moved to Cleveland to help some of his brothers operate a market on Kinsman Avenue, not far from Imperial. He stayed there until buying Imperial Beverage, a convenience store three doors down from 12205, from a brother in 2001.

He got to know the locals, many of whom stole from him.

"In terms of a bad neighborhood ranked from one to ten, it was a nine," Tayeh says. "And yeah, they stole, and I could never catch all of them."

He saw drug dealers keep coming into the neighborhood, and one day, Tayeh started to tip off the police. His tips helped put one dealer, Boobie, in jail for a while. Boobie got out, and one night, he came to see Sam.

"I was closing and had my car running. I used to be so nice to Boobie because I knew he was dangerous."

And he was. On this night, Boobie approached Tayeh on the slim piece of sidewalk between the store's front door and the running car and rubbed his gun all over his face. Tayeh jumped in his car and got away.

"Then another guy, Sean, knew I knew who he was, that he was selling," Tayeh says.

One night, Sean came in and slapped down a small package the size of a cigarette pack on the counter. It was a brick of crack. Tayeh called the police, 911, since Sean had just left the store and was in the area.

Five minutes later, Tayeh got a call back—not from the police, but from Sean.

"Why did you call the police on me?" Sean asked. He was not plaintive; he was threatening. Sean's cousin worked for the city's 911 dispatch office and had flipped on Tayeh, who gulped loudly.

"If you do that again, I will kill you," Sean said. Tayeh knew he meant it and that Sean had spared his life this time. This was really serious.

"Thank you," Tayeh said. He had grown up on the hardest streets of New York and Cleveland, and he was not a particularly humble man. But he was now terrified to find that a guy could easily get killed trying to improve a neighborhood.

Later, one night after work, Sowell came in for some beer and smokes.

"How can you take all the shit going down around here?" he asked Tayeh.

"It's bad; I do what I can to keep things together," Tayeh replied.

Anthony Sowell was good for the neighborhood, he thought.

Sowell, too, felt at home in the house and in the neighborhood. But what really excited him was a young lady named Lori Frazier, whom he met on a summer night near his bus stop.

Lori Frazier was a train wreck. In spring 2006, she was living on Forest Avenue, not far from Imperial, and had since 1989 rung up charges for eight drug-possession cases, solicitation, receipt of a stolen vehicle, drug trafficking, and escape from custody. She had given police three different birth dates and a home address for a place that was condemned, and she had variously called herself Lisa, Tharisa, and Thorisa Frazier. She had spent time in jail, on community supervision, and on probation. Lori was thirty-seven years old at the time and the mother of four children ranging in age from seven to nineteen, who were all in the custody of her mother, Eleanor Frazier.

Lori had been hospitalized for depression and other mental-health issues over the years; sometimes, voices in her head told her to run, to hurt herself, or to hurt others, reports showed.

Lori lived in squalor, turning tricks or whatever it took to score crack.

She was also the niece of then newly elected Cleveland Mayor Frank Jackson.

\* \* \*

Frank Jackson's political career was a study in government ladder climbing. Born in 1946 to George and Rose Jackson, the Cleveland native was one of five kids, four boys and a girl.

Jackson moved through the academic ranks with ease, earning his bachelor's, master's, and law degrees from Cleveland State University. He began his legal career as a night clerk for the Cleveland Municipal Court, then became an assistant city prosecutor. Jackson always cited the guidance of his mentor, Lonnie Burten (a Cleveland City Council member until his murder in 1984), as crucial to his career. Jackson won a spot on the council in 1989, serving on that panel until being elected mayor in 2005.

Jackson had married his wife, Edwina, in 1975, and by 2005, Jackson's family included two grandchildren and two great-grandsons.

Lori Frazier was Edwina's sister Eleanor's daughter.

It was a side of the family Jackson didn't publicly acknowledge, a sort of secret known but unspoken.

Lori Frazier was living six blocks from 12205 Imperial in the fall of 2005, a moving vagabond and a slight woman with a husky voice and a long, narrow face. Years of drug addiction had withered her frame until she was a wisp. Frail yet strong, Lori, whom friends called Lo, was a street-savvy opportunist.

She was just walking out of Jay's, a convenience store

on Buckeye Road and 116th Street, with a forty-ounce tucked into a brown bag. It was dark, around 8:30 P.M.

"I can get you something better than beer."

She looked at the man standing by a bus stop, leaning, looking at her. He was holding his own paper bag from a nearby Chinese takeout place. Anthony Sowell's line of patter wasn't glib or sweet. It was inviting and hit Lori just where she needed to be hit.

"What's your name?" Lori asked. Then the standard hooker-to-john line: "You like to party?"

The two looked at each other and realized a couple things: First, Sowell was no john. He was a guy who could get things she needed. And two, they were attracted to each other.

They headed to the Phase III, a beer and shot and whatever-you-want joint on Buckeye, right across from the bus stop. It was a brown-brick affair with no windows and a sign on the door that warned, "No handguns." The place was crowded, but they found a little table.

Sowell offered Lori some of his shrimp-fried rice.

"No, I just want to drink," she said.

After a couple of drinks, they headed over to the Sowell house on Imperial. Sowell was still living on the first floor, and the health ailments that would land Segerna in and out of the hospital were just beginning. She was still at the stage of being glad to have a man around the house. She put up with his occasional female visitors—and there were more than a few neighborhood girls who spent the night.

"I have to get up real early for work," he explained to

Lori as they settled into his room to work on the beer. "I work at Custom Rubber, at 55th and St. Clair."

That was okay, she said. They went to sleep early, and when she awoke, he was gone. She stayed for some time before heading back to the place where she was currently living. It occurred to her that she would be back, and soon.

"He was a nice guy, a really nice guy," Lori said later.

Lori came back the next night, and then the next. Days turned to weeks, and pretty soon, Anthony and Lori were a couple. He put up with her drug addiction. Sowell cooked for her; they partied; they went to the park. She moved into the house within weeks of their first meeting.

"It was our decision," Lori said. "I wasn't working, and every day except Sunday, he worked. Things were quiet. We went shopping for groceries together. He bought me clothes."

Sowell's ex-wife, Kim, and high school girlfriend, Twyla, had both called him Anthony, but Lori called him Tony.

He called her Lo.

Then, when Sowell's renovations were complete, they decided to move upstairs to the third floor, first living in a large sitting room at the front of the house, which opened onto a porch overlooking Imperial. Then they moved to a smaller bedroom at the rear of the house, with a window that had an inglorious view of Ray's Sausage, a neighborhood institution that manufactured meat products.

"When she came and started living at Anthony's, Lori was real nice. She'd come in, 'Hi, Sam,'" says Sam Tayeh, the beverage-store owner. "She was real clean and spoke very well."

Lori mostly watched television and smoked crack. Sometimes Sowell would just play video games while she got high, but he didn't partake, despite his previous dabbling in cocaine and his appreciation for good weed. He just didn't care about the crack back then, preferring to smoke Newport cigarettes and drink beer, sometimes maybe some wine.

He kept reasonably clean and even played chess with some of the neighborhood kids, including Bobby Doss.

"He sure didn't want anyone using crack around," Bobby's older sister Tanja Doss said. She had moved to Imperial Avenue shortly before Sowell got out of prison, across the street from 12205 Imperial. Sowell knew Tanja was a drug addict, but he had bonded with her one evening, before he met Lori Frazier.

"I was sitting on a bench, and he walked past, and we just started talking," she said. "He went to the store and got a twelve-pack; he was cooking out on his front porch."

They hung out, dated, she said, for a few weeks in summer 2005, before Tanja moved to New York to care for her sick mother, who had been left partially blind by a stroke. "Give me a call when you get there to let me know you're in safe," Sowell told her before she got on the bus to head out for Queens, New York, where her mother lived. She did, and they followed up with a few conversations after that. It was a fling, though. In the autumn of 2005, it became all about Lori Frazier.

In fact, when Tanja came back to visit her Cleveland friends and stopped by the Sowell house while in the neighborhood, Sowell came around from the side in answer to her knock on the front door.

"I can't come out; I have a girlfriend," he explained. Tanja was cool with it, but Lori, who was listening, heard her say something unsettling as she walked away.

"I'm gonna get him back."

It wasn't a threat so much as it was a girl who wanted Anthony Sowell, who was considered a prize by some girls.

But at this point Sowell wouldn't waver.

"He treated [Lori] so well," says Shelia Phillips*, a neighbor who lived nearby and clerked at Sam Tayeh's store in exchange for breaks on her rent.

"Tone and Lori would come into the store all the time; he was so good to her. And really a decent guy."

During the years that Anthony Sowell spent in prison, from 1990 to 2005, amazing technology strides were made. Portable phones, once only a possession of the wealthy, were now ubiquitous. Compact discs had replaced records and tapes and were now the most popular format

---

* Denotes pseudonym

to buy and sell music. And the Internet was now a haven for anyone seeking information or reaching out to make contacts.

Sowell had learned to keep up with developments as an electrician in the military, reading and rereading theory on repair and watching as new equipment was developed.

In other words, he was keen on this Internet thing. And it held something very important for him. He had been attracted to pornography for years, and now there was a whole new world of it available at one or two keystrokes. Shortly after setting up his apartment on Imperial, he furnished it with a battered, used computer. He became an avid Internet junkie like so many others attracted to emerging technologies. He paid his taxes online and enjoyed playing Internet chess.

Sowell also created a profile at Alt.net, a site for people with more unusual sexual proclivities. Dominance and submission, sadomasochism, and other sexual quirks that don't appear on the traditional sexual radar were all available on the meet-and-greet site, which also offered a chat room.

He named himself Tony 223936 and gave his audience a message:

"If your [sic] submissive and like to please, then this master wants to talk to you," he wrote on his Alt.com profile. "So get you're [sic] ass on over here NOW!"

He described his ideal partner as submissive and willing to "please . . . anytime, anyplace and anyway." He also described himself as a "performer," someone who "loves to be around people."

Several months later, Sowell also created an identity for himself on BlackPlanet, a social website that catered to African Americans. He listed himself as Anthony E and represented himself as single.

Sowell described himself as working in "manufacturing and production," said he'd attended Shaw High School from 1974 to 1977, and had "some college coursework completed" at Cleveland State College in 1985 and 1986. His favorite music was "slow jams," and his favorite TV show was *Ray*. His favorite web page was that of Kimora, host of the E! TV network's *Life in the Fab Lane*.

His head shot photo was the same on both websites and showed him in a gray knit cap and gray T-shirt, his PC visible on the right.

So although he was smitten with Lori, Sowell was also exploring another avenue of life, something that titillated him.

"He wanted to get a third person, a woman, into our sex," Lori said. "He wanted to watch; he wanted her to do me while he watched."

Lori, in love and not finding Sowell's request all that far out, talked among her friends and even offered a bit of money that Sowell promised. But when they found a taker, "all we did was just sit around and get high," Lori said.

So Sowell lived his life with Lori, his computer alter

ego, and his work. Relatively speaking, Sowell was a winner. He had some money, he had a girlfriend, and he was taking care of his elderly, sickly stepmother. He paid his rent. There was nothing out of the ordinary about him.

"In fact, people liked him," says Sam Tayeh. "But then he started to change."

# CHAPTER 4

Anthony, are you getting high?

**—TRESSA GARRISON**

There had always been a smell in the neighborhood of Imperial for as long as residents could remember. For decades, it was the savory smell of sausage being cooked at Ray's Sausage, a redbrick two-story building on the corner of Imperial and 123rd Street, next door to the Sowell house. Ray's Sausage was an institution, employing locals and selling both to vendors and walk-ins.

The business opened in October 1957, launched by Raymond Cash's father, and by 2006 was owned by Renee Cash and her brother, Raymond Jr. Their uncle was the famed Cleveland Indians first baseman Luke Easter, who himself had owned a sausage factory when he spent time in the minor leagues with the Buffalo Bisons.

In high school, Renee had handed out pencils with "Ray's Sausage" emblazoned on the yellow paint. It was a proud family carrying on a proud business.

The company prospered for decades, crafting head cheese and fresh beef and pork sausage, establishing a strong distribution network throughout northeast Ohio and extending to stores as far south as Columbus, places willing to pay for the extra freight for some of the good stuff.

The original Ray died in 1977, just as the neighborhood began its slow fade. Businesses shuttered, foreclosures jumped, crime increased. But although the family business teetered, it never faltered. Its inspection reports were always solid, and the product sold itself.

Raymond Jr., a gruff-voiced, gentle-natured man, had known the Sowell family for a long time, beginning with John Sowell, the grandfather.

"Thomas Sr. and John Sowell were master carpenters and painters, and they did a lot of work for us when we opened up," Renee Cash says.

"Thomas [Sr., Anthony's father] was my buddy," Ray said. "I used to go over there all the time." After Thomas died, in 2003, it was Ray who put new siding on the house for Segerna.

But by early 2006, Lori Frazier noticed a bad smell at 12205 Imperial, and it wasn't the sweet scent of Ray's. It was a sickly, putrid odor that filtered through the entire house, as if something had crawled somewhere and died.

And it wasn't just Lori who was smelling things; the Pompey family, renting space on the second floor, also became aware of the stench. First the Pompeys started seeing mice in their apartment several times a week. A pest exterminator was called, but it did no good. Then came the smell.

"There became a smell that I didn't recognize," Brandon Pompey said. "Maybe rotten food, if you will. . . . It would become stronger as you moved into the apartment. We speculated that a dead animal had crawled in there and died . . . It smelled like rotting fruit."

"It's Segerna, downstairs," Sowell said when Lori asked about it one day. His stepmother was becoming increasingly ill, her organs failing and her care requiring more work. Family members tended to her and she was hospitalized more and more.

Sowell gave Segerna's nephew, Jermaine Henderson, another excuse for the scent.

"He said it came from a flooded basement," Jermaine said. But most people, for some reason, just blamed Ray's Sausage next door.

"People assume it's us because we're in the meat business," Raymond Cash said. Eventually, residents complained to the district's city councilman, Zachary Reed.

"My office actually called the health department in 2007 to say that one of our residents called to say there's a foul odor across the street and it smells like a dead body," Reed said.

"He made us tear up the street, invest $25,000 to $30,000 for a new grease trap," Ray said of the councilman.

All told, the company would spend more than $20,000 on new vents and an updated exhaust system over the next four years.

The shop was inspected routinely for any sanitary violations as part of state and federal practice, and those inspection reports were all clean, showing no reason for a bad odor.

The grease trap replacement, along with cleaned and flushed drains on the street, didn't do it. Pouring bleach into the sewer outlet in the basement of the sausage place also didn't do anything to staunch the smell.

Finally, a local health department official determined that it was probably a dead animal trapped in an unfortunate, obscured location.

"He told us not to worry about it," Ray said.

The odor was palpable to people in the second-floor offices of the sausage shop, and employees would inhale the rancid smell as they walked up the steps, Renee Cash said. It was enough to force the business to keep the windows closed, even on the kindest of summer days.

Soon the nasty smell just became part of the landscape, one more thing that would add up, or not, to what was Anthony Sowell's world.


Sowell always knew where to score for Lori, even though she was quite capable of copping her own drugs. But Sowell, a jealous man, didn't want to run the risk of her selling her body for the drugs, and he didn't have the money to just hand over to her. He was savvy enough to know that the algebra of need—the drug user's equation that reads, "Need divided by supply equals use"—would sap his wallet.

Shortly after they met, though, "He started smoking," Lori said. "I told him if he started smoking, we weren't going to be together."

There are varying codes among drug users and their mates. Some users feel that to have a partner who also uses creates a friction that is untenable. Others are glad to have a partner in crime, someone who will cop and use with them.

For Lori, her code was clear; she cared enough for Sowell that she wanted him to be the one who stood straight in the face of her addiction because she knew where it would lead if he began to smoke crack. And it didn't take long to see she was right.

Lori came home one day and saw that Sowell was being secretive.

"What have you got?" Lori asked, looking at him. He stared back, blankly, then went down the stairs from the third floor apartment and out the front door. She knew there were going to be problems. She had been there before. And sure enough, shady characters began to come around the house, intruding on what was their safe place.

"He kinda turned on me," was how Lori put the evolving household dynamic over the next few weeks. The couple began to fight over drugs; who used more, who scored from whom. Hard drugs are a selfish endeavor by nature, prompting secretive and often combative behavior. The drug was often the love.

By June 2006, Sowell had quit paying rent to Segerna, who was complaining to friends and relatives. She asked him to leave but had little power to enforce her demand.

"She was trying to kick him out," says the younger Thomas Sowell. "But he just said he wouldn't leave."

Allan Sowell came by a couple of times, at his mother Segerna's request, to talk to Anthony about the rent, but he was never there.

Tressa would still come by and visit both her brother and her stepmother. Up to the third floor, down to the first.

"Anthony, are you getting high?" she asked him one day. There were signs; he was a little unkempt. He was tired. But he denied anything was going on. Tressa had distrusted Lori right away. She knew Lori was a drug user and that her brother was mostly a drinker.

"He was not smoking crack" until he met Lori, Tressa says. "He was just drinking until he fucked her. Her family helped out by keeping her kids. She couldn't even buy a pack of cigarettes. He rode buses with her so that she wouldn't go to crack houses. That's the kind of person he is. He likes to help people."

But he was digging the drugs now, just like Lori.

In the spring of 2006, Sowell hit what some in the neighborhood would have viewed as the lottery. Always wise in the ways of money, having made and managed a bit when he was in the military, Sowell got his tax return for those six months of full-time work for 2005. He had paid in but didn't make enough to pay out. He got back $3,000.

Sowell began looking for DVD players, CDs, clothes, and drugs. There was crack, pot, booze, girls. All day, all night, the party never stopped, and Lori was all of a sudden cast aside.

She came home one evening from her mom's after visiting her kids and found a full-on celebration in progress. The music could be heard down the street, and Lori came to the side door. She was met at the door by a young man she didn't recognize, who told her that Sowell wasn't there. Lori walked inside and couldn't believe what she saw. Kids as young as fifteen were inside the house dancing, listening to music, drinking cheap wine.

The party was out of control, and she turned into the mother that she was. She screamed at everyone. They didn't listen.

"I went downstairs, and there were girls hiding behind the furnace," Lori said. "I didn't know anyone there, and I left."

She went to her sister's place, not far from Imperial. She was heartbroken; even mired in her addiction, she could still feel. And she felt spurned in a very public way. It hurt. But she could forgive him. After all, she loved Anthony Sowell. He really was a good guy.

One morning in the summer of 2006, Lakeesha Pompey walked out to her car in the driveway of 12205 Imperial and knew it was time to move out when she found a scrap of T-shirt tied to the side mirror of her car. The material's placement was a sign to locals that it was okay to sell drugs at that house. People had been walking through the backyard, day and night. There had been a party or two, in the past month, but things were getting weird. Segerna was still battling health woes, although Lakeesha would see Virginia Oliver, Segerna's mother, over there almost every morning, having breakfast. It was a ritual. Sometimes Virginia came by bus, other times by the service shuttle for the elderly.

Once the Pompeys moved out, Anthony Sowell's third-floor apartment and Segerna's first-floor living space were separated by a whole empty floor in the huge house.

Lori moved back in shortly after that, but things weren't much better. She was arrested on October 3, 2006, for possession of crack, and three days later, Sowell secured the $1,000 bail for her. Although she had always given her mother's address as her home, for the first time, Lori told the court that she received mail at 12205 Imperial. It was comforting to her having a place she could get her court summons directly. And her mom, who was sick and dying, wouldn't have to know about her latest arrest.

A week later, on October 10, 2006, Lori was given a citation for having an open alcohol container in a car. She was riding with a friend on the way to score. She received a suspended sentence. Lori skipped her November 15 drug-charge hearing, and a warrant was issued for her arrest. They wouldn't find her for almost two years.

At home, she had something worse than the law to deal with. Sowell was raging, now that he was smoking crack, a drug known for inducing all kinds of aggression. It affected different people in different ways, but with Sowell, it made him crazy.

Now there were fights, physical scraps, between the two.

"Sometimes he would get so mad, so into his rage, he would scream and holler in my face," Lori said. "He smacked me and I fell on the table, and I tried to kick him. One time he told me he was gonna throw me out the window."

They would punch and scratch each other in drug-fueled battles. Still, she was never scared of him. She could hold her own anyway, but "he was getting high more and more" often with other people in the third-floor apartment. "I never went up there and got high with them," Lori said.

Eventually, Sowell threw Lori out, and she left; then he called and begged her to come back. Their chaotic relationship was headed nowhere fast, and neither one of them had any way to put on the brakes.

# CHAPTER 5

Overwhelming sense of loneliness and sadness and I
couldn't get away from it.

—ANTHONY SOWELL

February 2007 was the most frigid in Ohio in almost
three decades, with temperatures averaging nineteen
degrees. But most remarkable was the fifteen to twenty
inches of snow that swept through Cleveland starting the
second Tuesday of the month, and ending the next day,
the fourteenth.

Anthony Sowell was alone in his apartment after work,
Lori Frazier being back at her mother's during an "off"
part of their on-off relationship. Although he wasn't paying rent, Sowell still helped maintain the house on Imperial, and shoveling snow came with the territory. So he
bundled on his winter gear and went out to clear about
twelve feet of the front walkway; then he tackled the sidewalk. He wasn't feeling well—"I thought I had the flu,"
he later said—but went on with his chore. It took several
passes for him to get it all, and the snowfall was relentless.

The snow had shuttered the city; businesses had ground to a halt, and schools were closed the whole week. On Thursday the fifteenth, Sowell got up and began to walk over to his sister Tressa's, about four blocks away. On his way there, an older woman was doing her best to push a shovel to create a path from the sidewalk to her doorstep and her mailbox on the porch.

"Ma'am, you shouldn't be shoveling snow like that," Sowell told her.

"The post office said it wouldn't deliver my mail otherwise," the woman said.

Still feeling poorly himself, Sowell asked if she would allow him to do it. When he was done, he handed the shovel back to the woman, who thanked him profusely, and he continued on to his sister's house.

He walked in the door and immediately ran to the bathroom to throw up. Sowell had joked before about being around the germ-ridden flock of kids—nine in all— at Tressa's and how it increased his chance of coming down with something.

"I can't believe I can just walk in the door and get something," he kidded to Tressa when he came out of the bathroom. But it was much worse than he thought. He couldn't make it home. The subzero temperatures, the snow, and his rapidly diminishing health made him too weak.

Still, when the weather cleared, he went back to work, but his health hadn't improved.

"I kept on going to work and I was getting sicker and sicker," Sowell said. "I was taking Theraflu and stuff like that, still getting sicker. So just finally . . . my boss has been asking me about being sick and I told her, no, I was all right.

"And so I finally got really sick when I came in but I was determined to—I come in to work at six [A.M.]. Christine, which is the front office don't get in until eight, so I worked till eight and I stopped but at that time my body totally shut down. I couldn't—I could barely—I had to crawl up the steps almost and they called Chris over and Chris told me to go home but don't come back until I get well."

For days, Sowell tried to navigate the bureaucracy of the U.S. Department of Veteran's Affairs, where, he felt, he would receive the best health care available to a military veteran like himself. But between sleeping and arguing with the agency, which refused to admit him because he had lost his driver's license, Sowell kept fighting with what he still thought was the flu.

By Saturday, February 24, 2007, he had gotten replacement identification and headed on the Number 50 bus to the VA hospital. When it pulled up at the hospital, he fell out the door of the bus and onto the sidewalk.

He was taken into the emergency room, where doctors immediately found the problem: three arteries in his heart were clogged, two of them completely, and the other was 80 percent closed. Sowell's situation was too dire for the skeleton crew at the VA hospital, and he was ferried by ambulance to the Cleveland Clinic, home of some of the nation's best heart doctors.

They put him directly onto an operating table, but

despite their opening up the two completely closed arteries, it looked like it would be too late. Sowell had suffered a heart attack more than a week earlier, and there was damage. He was also suffering from atrial fibrillation, a condition in which the normal electric pulses of the heart are overtaken by abnormal pulses that speed the heart.

By Monday, February 26, Anthony Sowell was moved to the critical ward and was dying. He was given three stents first, a hope for stemming the damage to the front of his heart, which was essentially gone. A last resort was a pacemaker, but his overwhelmed heart couldn't take any more surgery. Instead, he was given a temporary pacemaker, which went through an opening in the neck. It saved his life.

Sowell was released a few days later, with a more common pacemaker in place, one that could also control his atrial fibrillation. He was also told that rehabilitation therapy was essential, to recondition his heart muscles, which were damaged.

He had no money for the rehab, though, and the VA wasn't going to pay.

"I was only sent to Cleveland Clinic on the VA [for] a heart problem, not the after care," Sowell said. "That bill alone was almost $200,000. I cannot—there's no way I could afford. And they wanted me to go to rehab every day of the week, from that morning to, basically eight hours. I said, number one, I wouldn't be able to pay for it. And number two, I would lose my job."

So he returned in March to Custom Rubber, walking through the door with a new pacemaker and a damaged heart. He lasted until July, when he began to have trouble breathing at work, and an ambulance had to come.

"That was the nail in the coffin," Sowell said. "It was the worst thing that could have happened. I got sick again after a heart attack. At work."

After eighteen months of working there, sometimes twelve-hour days and seventy-hour weeks, he left Custom Rubber on mutual agreement.

He applied for unemployment, and for the first time since he was released from prison, he was without a job. He had always worked, from being a paperboy and cutting lawns as a preteen to this point, July 2007.

What did he have now? An ailing stepmother, a girlfriend who seemed bent on leaving him—a departure he prompted with his uncontrollable violent behavior—a crack habit, and a lot of days with nothing to do. He was on Plavix, a beta blocker, and five aspirin a day.

Sowell also noticed little things that had changed with his life. He used to play chess on the computer and easily defeat the software. Now, he no longer could win, no matter how hard he tried.

"It affected me in all kinds of ways," Sowell says. "I could never do my old job as a machine operator, my coordination was off. Everything was off. I was sad, I must have had some kind of depression. There was just this overwhelming sense of loneliness and sadness and I couldn't get away from it."

* * *

In early 2007, Latundra Billups moved to Imperial Avenue and was surprised to run into her old friend Lori Frazier, while on the way to a local store. The two women had grown up together for a time in the city's Fifth Ward, both kids with potentially decent futures.

Latundra was a military brat who'd graduated as a sixteen-year-old from an elite Catholic boarding school with a life full of promise. She had spent her childhood in exotic places like Germany, Hawaii, and California. There was no reason to expect her not to succeed. Her parents split when she was still in high school, and she and her sister moved in with her mother after she got out of school. She got a job as an inspector at Avon Cleaners, a family dry-cleaning business that had promise for a future for her.

"Except that there were the drugs I fell into, all my fault," she says. "There were so many fun things for me to do, and I was older. I got a boyfriend and had three children by the time I was twenty. . . . I had a bad point by 2002. I had five felonies, and then I caught a drug-trafficking case with my kids' father."

She was in and out of prison: eighteen months here, a year there.

"And when I got out in 2004, I was all the way downhill. My kids were taken away and lived with my mom. I was an alcoholic crackhead."

Lori, four years older than Latundra, was well into her own habits. The two caught up quickly and found they had more in common now than they had as kids—lengthy criminal records and a love of crack.

The two would go over to Latundra's place and score—"I was dealing with someone who had drugs"—and hang around and get high.

Latundra didn't go over to the house on Imperial much at that time. She liked Sowell—she called him Tone and he called her La La—but he was taken. She did notice that he and Lori fought a lot. But she just figured it was the drugs.

Like Latundra Billups, Crystal Dozier knew just about everyone in the Mount Pleasant neighborhood. She was tight with Lori Frazier, to start. The two had gone to elementary school together. Crystal had never been to the house on Imperial, but she had sure walked past it enough times. Lori had seen her in the neighborhood, buying crack.

Crystal never came home on the night of Mother's Day, May 13, 2007. At thirty-five, she wasn't known for her punctuality, nor was it unheard of for her mother or her sister not to hear from her for a few days. But her mother, Florence Bray, had a bad feeling this time. Crystal had walked a hard road, made trickier to navigate by her own mistakes.

But, like Latundra, there had been a time when a pre-teen Crystal had had a chance. She'd gone to school as much as she could stand, and her parents gave her a decent home. Born in 1971, Crystal was the second of four kids.

The family lived in the Imperial area at a time when the neighborhood was still relatively safe, and the people who lived there took care of their property.

Crystal played dress up, and she enjoyed it when people paid attention to her. She liked to sing; she liked to cook. But she also liked to get high.

She was thirteen when she got pregnant for the first time. The father was seventeen. She got pregnant again at fourteen. The father was twenty. The future was not so bright after that. (By the time she was thirty-five, she had seven children by three different men.)

Crystal soon dropped out of school, and her parents divorced. Her mom, Florence Dozier, took the kids and moved to East Cleveland. Although the area was going down fast, she hoped the change would help Crystal.

Instead, the young girl dug in her heels and rebelled. She moved in with the father of her second child.

"He coaxed her into running away. I couldn't eat; I couldn't sleep," Florence remembered. "I sat outside; I walked up and down the streets looking for my child. That's a scary, hurting feeling. I was a wreck. I didn't know where my child was; I didn't know if she was all right. She was afraid of him. After he won her over . . . he coaxed her into doing stuff, and she did it. He had total control over her."

Crystal eventually married a fellow seven years older than her named Anthony Troupe, records show, and the two moved into a place on Bessemer, not far from the neighborhood. Over the years, she gave each of her children names that started with an *A*, a curious habit that made sense somewhere deep in her soul. She was lost and getting more so.

In 1987, Crystal and her husband were deemed unfit parents by a social worker, who claimed that her oldest child, Anthony Dozier, then three, "has marks on his body from beatings." He was removed from the home, and his brothers and sisters followed him into a maze of foster care.

Then there was Crystal's long list of arrests.

She had arrests for drug possession, theft, and receiving stolen property and did some jail time. In 1990, she was pulled over for a routine traffic violation, then didn't show up for her court appearance. It happened repeatedly, eventually turning a misdemeanor into an arrest warrant. One time, she used her daughter's name, Annette Bell, in an effort to keep from having her real identity known. (That later gave the real Annette Bell a helluva time trying to clear her name.)

Crystal's husband, Anthony Troupe, also had legal trouble. Drug possession, domestic violence. Even her mother, Florence Dozier, had problems with the law. She was arrested two days after Christmas 1991 and charged with drug possession. She briefly served time in 1993, then was arrested again shortly after her release on theft charges. In June 2002, she received a ticket for open liquor in a car, then failed to show up for her court hearing. She settled the case in 2006, records show.

Although Crystal stayed in touch with her oldest two children, she never managed to get the family together. Her four youngest daughters were adopted by one family.

Her son Andre was adopted by a foster mother but died at age eleven from complications of asthma, relatives said.

Her oldest child, Anthony Dozier, enlisted in the U.S. Marines at the age of eighteen in 2003, and he would come home on leave every year. And each time, it would be apparent that his mother had not licked drugs. He would see her only "if I could find her," he said.

He was able to find her in April 2007, and was pleased. "She was doing really good, had a boyfriend . . . who she was staying with and from my understanding was off drugs and doing very well."

On Mother's Day, Crystal called her mother to wish her a happy Mother's Day. They shared a laugh about their lives.

Crystal also took a call that day from her daughter Antonia. They talked for a while and said good-bye.

Then Crystal was gone.

Anthony Dozier came home again later that month and went over to Crystal's house on Mount Auburn, about a mile from Imperial, then headed over to the Fourth District police station.

The station, on Kinsman, not far from Imperial on the city's southeast side, was the city's busiest by far. It served the poorest people in Cleveland, and it had the most calls. There was a constant rotation of patrol units on the street at any given time, but there was also an office front where the public could come in to file complaints or reports.

"When I filed the police report, I went to the station and told them everything that happened . . . they sent a patrol car to the house where she was staying," Anthony said. "Then I had talked to someone she had known, an ex-girlfriend, who said there was a house on 130th . . . a known drug house or some guy who sold drugs to her."

He told the police about the house, and they went up there and talked to folks at the address. When Anthony Dozier went back to the police, they told him he would get a report in three days.

The report never arrived.


In June 2007, the temperatures rose, and neighbors in the Imperial Avenue area again began to raise a furor over the stink. Calls began to come in to the office of Ward Two City Councilman Zachary Reed, who dispatched his own staff to survey the area, which lay in his jurisdiction.

"We received a phone call from a resident that said a foul odor came across the street and it smells like a dead person, not dead meat, not a dead animal. A dead person," Reed said.

He called the city health department, which sent someone out to the area. It was then that the city asked Ray Cash Jr., the owner of Ray's Sausage, to replace the grease traps in his building. He did. The smell continued. Visits from the city also continued for a while, men in white city cars wearing city badges. But nothing changed. The smell continued as the summer heat burnished itself into the air.

The same month, Sam Tayeh, the owner of Imperial Beverage, continued to smell the odor as well. His wife was working at the store, but the smell got too overpowering, and she refused to come back.

One morning in June 2007, Tayeh came to the store to find an employee, Jeff Beacon, waiting for him. Beacon was a fiftysomething local who had his share of hard luck, but who worked hard.

"Come out here and look at this," he said, motioning to the Dumpster in the small area behind the store.

At first, Tayeh resisted. "I don't care what's out there; just get to work."

"No, really, you need to see this," Beacon insisted.

Together, they walked to the Dumpster and Sam peeked in. There, two packages, each about five feet long and wrapped in duct tape, took up a good portion of the container. Flies buzzed around the packages, and the smell was sickening.

"I went inside to think about this," Tayeh says. "Then I thought that the girl who lived upstairs had a dog, a pretty big dog. So I went up there and asked if her dog was okay."

Yes, the dog was fine.

The smell was stultifying and getting worse. The garbage pickup would come later in the day. Tayeh instructed Beacon to pour some bleach in the Dumpster. It helped. The Dumpster was emptied that afternoon. Problem solved, for now.

About the same time, Segerna Sowell's nephew, Jermaine Henderson, came by Imperial. He would do odd jobs when Anthony Sowell couldn't get to them, and in this case, some siding had come loose near the front of the house. It was an easy job, he figured, looking at the flapping piece. He needed some kind of cement or adhering substance. It would be in the basement, which served as a catchall for home-improvement materials and tools, given the lack of space in the backyard for a shed.

Jermaine went to the side door, which provided the only access to the basement, and found it locked—no surprise, in a neighborhood where crime was an issue. Jermaine knocked on the door, which was solid wood at the bottom with a window on top. There were curtains on the window from the inside.

He got no response, and cupping his hands, he peered inside. Wedged between the door and stairs was a snow shovel.

"I knew he had to be in there," Jermaine said. "And I could not get in there with it like that."

He began to holler to get Sowell's attention, now curious "and a little scared" at seeing the shovel and the blocked door. It had to be intentionally placed there to keep people out. Why would Sowell want to keep people out? What was he doing in there?

Finally, he gave up. The siding would have to wait.

After his heart attack, 2007 was a time of recovery for Sowell—and a time of indulgence for Lori Frazier. She would be gone for days, weeks. Sometimes she came back for a few days, then left again. She felt it was more and more taxing to spend time there.

On occasion, Sowell would get calls from her children, looking for their mother.

"Have you seen my mommy?" would come the voice, defeated and sad. "Is my mommy there?"

And when Lori would come back from wherever she had been, he had to ask her: "How do you think I feel when your kids call for two or three days straight and I don't know where their mommy is?"

Sowell was now using drugs, too, although he and Lori didn't use together all that often. She was as careful as she could be, knowing that the outstanding warrant for her arrest was for a drug-possession felony and realizing that the court would not be generous with her for skipping her court appearance.

In addition to collecting his unemployment checks, Sowell had found a new job with new hours. He was working as a scrapper, mining abandoned buildings for copper, empty cans, aluminum, and any other metals that could bring a buck from places like Ohio Metal Recycling or Cleveland Scrap.

He became a routine sight among the transient gaggle of raggedly dressed, beaten-down denizens of the area, shoving rusted grocery carts pilfered from foreclosed and shuttered homes and businesses.

"Everybody knew him," said Kim Kemp, a local girl and also sometime scrapper. She also knew Sowell's habits, down to his drug use. "He smoked. I guess he did what he did to get his hustle."

By Thanksgiving 2007, things seemed to be well, though. Virginia Oliver came over to visit her daughter,

Segerna, and Anthony and Lori came down, and everyone watched TV for a while, talking and enjoying their time together.

"I didn't know [Lori Frazier's] name, but I knew who she was related to—the mayor," Virginia said. "She seemed to be a nice girl. She told me her mom was sick."

Virginia asked her if she had a job, and "that's when we stopped talking."

At the time, Virginia also smelled something, perhaps a dead animal. "I think we had an exterminator in," Virginia said.

Between smoking crack and his scrapping routine, Sowell began to lose a lot of weight. His once-stout frame was gaunt, and his face was changing, becoming drawn. His hands were dirty, and he too smelled, a mixture of the same odor that permeated the neighborhood in the summer and mustiness, like old clothes.

And one night Lori came into the Imperial Beverage store with bruises on her neck.

"What happened to you? Are you all right?" Sam Tayeh asked, looking at the dark bruises on each side of her throat.

"I'm getting rid of that motherfucker," Lori told him. "I'd call the police but I can't because I have warrants."

The year 2007 ended unceremoniously. But 2008 was the beginning of the end.

# Chapter 6

I cried the whole weekend.

**—ANTHONY SOWELL**

One day in early 2008, Lori Frazier came home to the house on Imperial and found a bloody mess.

There was blood on the walls, on the floor, and on the bed, although it looked like Sowell had done a noble job of trying to clean it up. It also looked like he had a hole in the side of his head.

"Someone tried to rob me," Sowell told her, though he was evasive when Lori pressed him for details. But she had enough trouble. Her mother, Eleanor, was getting sicker and sicker with cancer, and Lori was starting to scale back her own drug use. She wasn't carousing or hustling, and she wasn't spending as much time at the house on Imperial.

Downstairs at the house, Segerna was getting sicker as well. Her kidneys were failing, and she was on the list for a kidney transplant. She was fortunate to be in a city so well endowed with stellar medical help, thanks to the Cleveland Clinic, one of the premier health-care operations in the world.

It seemed every time Lori stopped by Imperial, there was something new going wrong with Sowell.

In late February, she came by, and Sowell's neck was "torn up down to the white meat," she recalled. He told her he had been attacked while in a vacant house, scrapping. He said he'd been deeply scratched during the fight. It wasn't long after that Lori encountered Sowell just home from the hospital after getting stitches to close a wound to the right side of his throat, which he said had happened on his way back from nearby Woodland Hills Park. He was nonchalant about the attack, despite his injury.

"Who was this, who was attacking you?" Lori pressed. She was both worried for his safety and alarmed at his reluctance to tell her.

"I killed the motherfuckers," Sowell told her. "You don't gotta worry 'bout those motherfuckers; I killed 'em."

The injuries were also hindering Sowell's ability to look for work, which he was still doing, although with no success. He went to a place that had helped him before, Towards Employment, an employment agency that specialized in placement for ex-offenders. But whereas he'd been well received the first time, coming in with clothes pressed and a neat appearance, now Sowell looked beat up and unkempt.

"I saw him have a weight loss and not look as healthy as he initially did," said Deborah Lucci, a placement agent at Towards Employment.

He claimed that he had been beaten up by his girlfriend. In his file, there was placed a note: "He has a stalker and she is related to the mayor."

Sowell's elusiveness with Lori about the injuries was compounded by some changes at the house. She still cared about the place, even though she wasn't living there.

One day, she noticed the door to the front sitting room was closed, and she walked over and tried to open the door.

"What you doing, what you doing?" Sowell said, running down the hall. The door was locked. That door was never locked. The sitting room of the third floor overlooked Imperial and had a small window at the front, allowing some light in. Two bedrooms were located on each side of the hallway leading to the living room. The room Sowell and Lori used—now just Sowell—abutted the living room but had no door between the two rooms. It seemed as if he were hiding something in that front room. As it turned out, he was.

Lori thought it was "strange . . . all this stuff happening, windows broken, him all cut, seemed like every time I was seeing him he was all cut up."

"Are you getting high still?" she turned and asked him one day. She had already seen the stem, a hollow chamber used to smoke crack, on his dresser.

"No," he responded. And he asked her to leave.

* * *

On March 6, 2008, Lori Frazier's warrant caught up with her, big-time. She was caught in a car with a crack pipe. It wasn't a relapse, exactly, because she hadn't really given it all up, try as she might. It was the beginning of the end, as they say.

Lori tried to give a fake name to the officer—Tharisa Frazier—but it was her time to go. She went back to the Cuyahoga County Corrections Center, a place she knew well. In fact, Lori knew the judicial system incredibly well. She had been on probation, done community service, and escaped fines only because she was constantly declared indigent.

Now she was in the county lockup, and that was about it.

This is when Anthony Sowell made his move to prove his love.

It's said that reaction is often more telling than action, and if so, Sowell's reaction to Lori's incarceration was indicative of some heart and soul. Yes, he was on drugs, and he was abusive, and he could be violent to Lori.

"Nobody in her family visited, nobody, but me," Sowell said. "I was there three times a week sometimes and I wasn't working. I would walk all the way from my house . . . to save a little money. I put it on her books," he said, meaning that he credited the money he'd saved by walking to Lori's prison account. "Sometimes I had money to go, but when I didn't I didn't miss no days."

Lori got out on Wednesday, April 23, posting a $1,000 personal bond; no bondsman would take the risk on her. Sowell had come up with the money.

Despite Sowell's generosity with the bond, Lori didn't come back to Imperial. She moved to a small house in Twinsburg, twenty miles south, where some relatives of hers were renting. She was worn out with Sowell, although she would still occasionally come by the house on Imperial.

But she wasn't able to keep things together, and they were moving fast now.

On May 28, 2008, she blew off her court date, and another warrant came her way. She was arrested again June 25.

This time, she made her court date. And this time, Sowell came down to the courthouse with her.

As he sat in the gallery, he watched the parade of people who had made a mess of their lives.

"I just met her lawyer that morning when I got there," Sowell said. "They called her out a little . . . after that and she went in front of the judge. This lawyer and judge knew each other. It was going bad for her."

But Lori's attorney pulled it off. He told the judge that Lori's boyfriend had come in. No one ran Anthony Sowell's background; no one knew he was a sexual violator with fifteen years of penitentiary time behind him. On that day, he was the hero, the guy who cared.

Judge Nancy McDonnell called on Sowell to come forward, and he testified on Lori's behalf.

"I got up there in front of the judge and told her that

[Lori] got people," Sowell said. "I told her I love her, I'm always there for her and she got people who care . . .

"I was getting ready to cry. But that turned the tide for her. The judge put her on probation, strict probation."

It was August 2008.

Lori was battling demons that got louder and louder. She was confused by the different Sowell, the one who loved her, then appeared with horrible cuts and was in her face, angry at her with shaking rage.

She was fighting the relentless tug of intoxication. She missed her mom. She loved her kids.

It was no wonder the court sent her for mental-health counseling after her hearing. She had been diagnosed with depression in 1998 after her father's death, then received outpatient mental-health care in 2002, then was hospitalized for mental disorders that same year. She said she heard voices that told her to hurt herself.

Now Lori was found to have a depressive disorder and given a prescription for Paxil. She took it for a while, but "it made me jittery," she said.

She went back to Imperial with Sowell for a few nights. The court had given her a list of phone numbers to call if she felt suicidal at any point, and Sowell kept the list for her. At one point, she did call, with Sowell overseeing it.

"They asked her did you feel like you're going to kill yourself or hurt someone," Sowell said. When she said yes, she hung up rather than wait for a response. The emergency hotline called back immediately, and Sowell held them off.

"No, she's just pissed off; she's not serious about hurting herself," he explained. Lori left in the morning, and the hotline called back. The worker wanted to know if Lori had gone back into a place where she could get some help. Sowell had no answer.

"I don't know," he said. "She's not here."

In fact, she was leaving him for good, she again claimed.

She had heard that despite his protestations of love for her, Sowell was messing around with other girls.

"When she got out of jail, she didn't wanna go back at all with him; she didn't like Tone anymore," says Latundra Billups, one of Lori's close friends who had spent hours getting high with the couple over the past year.

This part of the end of the relationship was a drawn-out event with plenty of acrimony and name-calling and accusations. And the accusations were rough.

"One day they had this big argument, I was over there, and she was calling him a rapist," Latundra says. "The next day they were back together."

But shortly after that, Lori moved out for good, leaving some of her clothes behind.

It was a Friday in August 2008 when she left for good. The on-again, off-again relationship had simply fallen apart over the past year. Sowell's behavior—the furtiveness and his increasing agitation—had taken its emotional toll. It was a big deal for Sowell, who would later say the break brought out feelings of anger that he couldn't control.

"I cried the whole weekend" after she left, Sowell said.

Lori left the neighborhood and refused to answer anyone's calls for three days. On the third day, Sowell went by Latundra's apartment with three garbage bags. He said they were Lori's clothes and asked that she give them to Lori when she next saw her.

"A couple days later, Lori came over to pick up the bags," Billups says. "She told me that her clothes were in there. And they were cut into little pieces."

Segerna Sowell, who had been staying with her mother for months, got a kidney transplant in August. She would never return to Imperial to stay. She left her first floor in its typically immaculate condition. She had decorated it in a beige and white color scheme. The large sofa and matching love seat were beige, and the room featured a round, light brown rug; beautiful wooden-framed mirrors; tchotchkes sitting on built-in shelves; and on one wall, a painting of Thomas Sowell, her late husband.

The kitchen, too, displayed Segerna's simple tastes, with a small, round glass-top table in the middle and a wood-paneled cabinet, a white electric stove, and a brown Frigidaire.

Scattered throughout the dwelling were framed photos of family members, including Sowell.

In the coming days, weeks, and months, Jermaine Henderson, Segerna's nephew, would come by sometimes, checking on the house and, once in a while, partying a little bit.

Twelve years younger than Sowell, Jermaine also had a long criminal record, spending time in state prison on various charges including witness intimidation, kidnapping, aggravated burglary, and receiving stolen property. On the street, they called him "J," but he handed cops all kinds of names, like Jezel Michaels or Edward Stevenson.

# CHAPTER 7

We were praying that she was doing drugs—
you can fix that.

**—SHANNON LICCARDO**

While things had coalesced to end Sowell's relationship with Lori, the neighborhood was enduring a wave of disappearances.

On February 12, 2008, LeShanda Long called her father, Jim Allen, on his cell phone.

"Do you know what day it is?" she asked him.

"No, it seems like there's something, but I can't remember," Jim said. And LeShanda giggled. She had once been a little girl, after all, and sometimes it seemed all she wanted to do was to curl up and return to that world of innocence.

"It's your birthday," LeShanda said.

It was a game father and daughter had long played. Jim Allen was a corrections officer for Cuyahoga County, and although his daughter had seen more trouble in her twenty-four years than he cared to acknowledge, he loved her like any solid parent would. She was his baby.

Still, when LeShanda disappeared, in May 2008, there was no one who really paid attention. She had been hanging out with a boyfriend, a ne'er-do-well named Reggie. But LeShanda would split on him sometimes and be gone for weeks. And her dad—well, it would be months between calls or visits.

LeShanda was born in Cleveland to Jewell Long, who was plagued by her own drug addiction and criminal behavior. Her raps included criminal trespass and drug possession. Jim Allen lived with the kids and his grandmother, trying the best he could. Jewell's sister Caroline Long was also in the picture.

"[LeShanda] was controlling and she had all these boys around, brothers and relatives, she would always try to get to do what she wanted," Jim said. "They would sit on her and hold her down." And when she didn't get her way, she cried, and they dubbed her Crybaby Gangster.

But in 1990, a social worker paid a visit to the house on Folsom, about five miles from downtown, and found six kids between the ages of one and thirteen, including LeShanda, home alone. Records show that Jim's grandmother had asked the county several times to find the children a home because she could not give them the care they needed.

But it took the visit to make that happen. LeShanda and the rest of the kids were headed for foster care, but their aunt Caroline rescued them, taking all six kids into her home to join her own two sons. She worked at a gas station to help pay the bills.

"That is what you are supposed to do for family," she said. "In my heart, it wouldn't have been right if they all were separated."

Caroline moved them around, first to the Cleveland suburbs and then to the smaller village of Kokomo, Indiana, where she got a job at a nursing home, and the kids got a new start. But that's when LeShanda started acting up.

"It got to a point to where she would stay out and not let me know where she was," Caroline said. "She kept saying she wanted to be with her mother and father. So one day, I told her if her daddy wanted her back, she could go back home."

So back to Cleveland LeShanda went, along with her ever-growing shadow of rebellion and defiance.

"I was always part of her life," Jim said. "But I couldn't be there always."

At one point, LeShanda lived with Jim and his new wife. But she kept running away. Her father reported her missing numerous times, and she would always be found, in trouble. At thirteen years old, LeShanda already had her first child, one of three she would have by the time she reached seventeen. She was picked up for theft and for taking her children away from relatives, who'd been given custody after LeShanda was declared unfit.

Starting at age fifteen, she was in and out of juvenile jail and psychiatric care. She spent six months attending

drug and alcohol counseling classes at Applegate, a
national drug-treatment chain.

"It was like AA," Jim said. "You come in and talk and
discuss and have questions and answers."

But nothing worked. At sixteen, LeShanda found herself once more locked up in juvenile detention in Cleveland. In October 2000, she wrote the first in a series of
letters to Cuyahoga County Juvenile Judge John W. Gallagher.

She asked to be moved to one of several esteemed
homes or schools for troubled kids: Summit Academy, in
Herman, Pennsylvania; Marycrest, in Independence,
Ohio; Parmadale Institute, in Parma, Ohio; or Day Break,
an anger-management treatment center with a location
in Cleveland.

"Sir, I am sixteen and I have two daughters," she
wrote. "I can honestly say at the rate I'm going I'll be
dead before I'm eighteen."

LeShanda said she was not asking to go home but
simply for help in finding a place that could give her
in-patient care that would stick.

"I've been to Scioto four times and not once has it
helped me," she said. Scioto Juvenile Correctional Facility, located just north of Columbus and operated by the
state's Department of Youth Services, is a hard-core
lockup for young people in deep trouble. LeShanda fit
the bill. She was pregnant with her third child.

So back to Scioto it was.

She took group-therapy sessions, had victim's-aware-
ness counseling, took a computer class, and learned weld-

ing. She was preparing to take her GED and applied to take the SAT exam.

She again wrote the judge in January 2001 asking for an early release so she could attend the local community college for a couple years before transferring to Spellman College or Georgia Tech in Atlanta, Georgia.

Among her goals upon release, she said, were to "be a good mother and role model to my children."

LeShanda got out but failed miserably to meet these goals over the next few years. She was arrested repeatedly, with charges including hitchhiking and disorderly conduct, and her father was sure she was using drugs.

"Yes, she was probably was on drugs," Jim said. He had been to places she lived and "seen her and seen the way she acted. You know your child, you know when something's not right. Her swagger, her tone, her different mind-set. It alters a person."

Jim and other relatives had custody of LeShanda's kids. She would disappear for a few months and then reappear. She was erratic and living a hard street life.

In 2007, LeShanda was twenty-three and had an apartment near Imperial and 123rd Street, spitting distance from the Sowell house. She was living there off and on with a boyfriend. Reggie was the only name Jim knew him by. LeShanda was distant, lost.

In late February 2008, the hospital called Jim Allen to report that LeShanda had been beaten up and was being treated for her injuries. He went to get her.

"It's time for you to come out of the streets," he told his daughter. Although LeShanda's temper made her a force to be reckoned with on the street, she was only four feet seven and 100 pounds, a slight girl. He was afraid for her now.

She came home to live with him once more, and Jim began to understand that his daughter was going to have to live on the system. She just didn't have the strength to make it with a regular job.

"I was going to show her step-by-step how to get adequate housing and get on welfare and relief to help herself somehow," he said. He took her to the Social Security office to get a Social Security card.

"At first, she was receptive," he said. "Then, the light-bulb went off."

After she left his house one May afternoon and headed back toward her place on Imperial, he never saw her again. It was as if she disappeared into the sidewalk cracks.

On any given day, it seemed, a cop could pluck a denizen out of the Imperial Avenue neighborhood, run him or her for warrants, and get a hit.

On May 21, 2008, Tishana Culver became one of those many when she walked out on her work-release program. She was serving time on a domestic-violence conviction in 2006, having first put in some state prison time before a jammed system set her into a looser program. On June 20, a warrant was issued, and a judge charged her with upper-level escape, a second-degree felony.

Her last known address was 12317 Imperial. But no

one really cared to look too hard. She would turn up somehow.

Tishana was born in 1978 to unwed high school sweethearts who split up before her first birthday. Her mom, Yvonne Williams, moved in with her own mother and took Tishana with her. Her dad, Sam Culver Jr., got into serious criminal trouble, spending more time in and out of courtrooms and jails than with his daughter. In 2001, he was sentenced to ten years for aggravated robbery as a repeat offender.

By junior high, Tishana was prone to fights with her peers. She had the first of her six children during her sophomore year at John Adams High School and never stuck with the father. She graduated, however, and started working in cosmetology. Tishana did her best to take care of her growing brood of children.

In the mid-1990s, Tishana met a young man named Marcus Johnson. Friends said they planned to get married, but in 1998, he was found with a bullet in his head in the city's Gordon Park, on the Lake Erie waterfront. He had killed himself.

It's apparent, looking at police records, that Tishana plunged into problems almost immediately after Marcus's suicide, racking up criminal charges for drugs, weapons, and prostitution.

By 2000, she was twenty-two, had three children, no husband, and an escalating drug habit.

That year, she hooked up with Carl Johnson (no relation to Marcus), who became a significant presence in her life.

They were both deep into drugs. He worked at a bowling alley; she worked the streets.

"Whenever she put that red lipstick on, I knew what it meant," Carl Johnson said. "Unless I tied her down, there was no way I could stop her. I hated to watch the person I love hop in and out of cars."

They rarely stayed in the same places for long, moving around from rented rooms and apartments to the spare rooms of relatives.

She had three more kids with Carl.

In 2006, she caught the domestic-violence charge after punching Carl and attempting to stab him after he tried to keep her from going out on the streets. This time, she was sent to prison.

When Tishana walked out on the work-release program, she tried to come home to the place on Imperial, but her mom and sister, who lived there with Tishana's children, didn't want the kids to see the train wreck their mother had become. It was tough love to the nth degree.

The last time Tishana Culver was seen was by the authorities when she checked out for the day on Wednesday, May 21, 2008.


In October 2008, yet another woman around the Imperial area fell off the face of the earth, and this time, it was easy to track: forty-four-year-old Michelle Mason just quit using the $1,000 of social-services money that was direct-deposited into her account at the start of every month.

She left her mother's house, the same one she'd

grown up in, on October 8 around 10 A.M. and headed to take the bus back to her apartment, about three miles away.

Her apartment was a portion of a rooming house, actually, but she was happy to have anything. Her life had been hard, and she was fragile.

To start with, Michelle was five feet seven yet weighed all of 85 pounds, a stick figure of a woman. She was bipolar, HIV positive, and took a small pharmacy's worth of pills in order to function. She'd survived being shot and left for dead in a garage, after which she had crawled to a nearby market—the incident happened about one-half mile from the family home—and got help. She now had a glass right eye.

Yes, life had been a long, hard ride for Michelle.

She'd left home for New York in 1979, when she was sixteen, then came back five years and two children later. She also came home carrying the AIDS virus, which she'd contracted through sharing a needle with fellow heroin addicts.

Her criminal record in the Cleveland area was a full one—seven of her nine county cases were drug related—as well as a breaking and entering and a soliciting after a positive HIV test.

But in 2001, she'd turned it around. At least that's what most everyone thought. Michelle had been sentenced to attend three meetings of drug and alcohol counseling a week, and she'd stayed with it, even going to outpatient drug treatment at Marymount Hospital, near her mom's house.

"She was standing up and giving talks at the AA meetings," says her son, Shannon Liccardo. She was trying.

But then there were backslides.

Michelle was popped twice in 2003 for soliciting, and about three months before she disappeared in October 2008, she had been arrested for disorderly conduct. She was fined $80 for that arrest, which she never paid. She didn't have time to, because she was gone.

The family managed to get an item in the local newspaper on December 1, 2008, announcing a rally for Michelle. It noted that she suffered from a bipolar condition and had not been heard from since October 8. The 107-word blurb noted that Michelle disappeared after meeting a sexual predator who had been in prison for 18 years. The gathering was held at East 116th Street and Buckeye, a mile from the Sowell house on Imperial.

Few people showed up, disheartening everyone involved.

The family knew that the guy Michelle had recently been hanging out with was a sex offender, and they thought it would be common sense to search the man's place, her son, Shannon Liccardo says. But family members were told there were "jurisdictional issues" regarding such a search, and there was no evidence he had anything to do with Michelle's disappearance.

"They talked about rights that he had, as well," Shannon says. "But if I raped someone, my rights should be limited. But the police didn't see it that way."

But as family and friends distributed flyers, Shannon had another way to track his mother. On the first weekday of every month, his mother would get up early because that was the day her social-services check would hit her bank account. The first thing she would do is take care of her phone bill and get some groceries.

On November 3, the money was untouched. Same on December 1. That's when he knew that something was definitely wrong.

"We were praying that she was doing drugs," Shannon says. "You can fix that."

After the January 2, 2009, check was not tapped, he called social services and asked that they put a hold on the checks. The family had no idea what had happened to Michelle Mason.

Around the same time Michelle Mason went missing, Lori Frazier got a job at Charley's Grilled Subs in the Tower City Center, in downtown Cleveland. Getting a job was a requirement of her probation. She also submitted to drug testing and visited with a counselor. Lori made all her appointments. The odd man out was Anthony Sowell, who was not cleaning up his act.

In fact, he was getting worse, both physically and emotionally.

"His face changed," his sister Tressa Garrison said. "He would be up all night, then some more all day."

And the smell, man, the smell.

It was starting to come through the vents at Sam Tayeh's store, across the street. He was dumping Clorox, Pine-Sol, whatever he could, around access points to the store. And the same smell was coming off Sowell when he came into the store.

"He gave me a headache from the smell," Tayeh says. "It was overpowering."

He also noticed that Sowell's movements were changing, from slow and calm to furtive and abrupt.

"I would see him walk down the street, and he was very paranoid. He would walk and keep looking behind him. Mentally, he wasn't the same character."

And Sowell's buying habits, well, they changed, too. In addition to his normal purchases—the forty-ounce bottles of King Cobra malt liquor, Newport cigarettes, and lighters (four or five at a time), the typical crack user supply—now he wanted electrical extension cords and plastic bags.

"Not the regular plastic garbage bags," Tayeh says. "He asked for the heavy-duty bags. He bought five boxes at one time—$3.89 a box."

Tayeh thought it was for yard work, since he'd seen Sowell puttering around in the yard as the warm weather faded. He had cleaned up the backyard, in fact. Small as it was, there was some decent grassy area there when the garbage was picked up. Just open ground, enough to plant something. Or bury it.

# CHAPTER 8

Bitch you can scream all you want, you're fixin' to die.

**—ANTHONY SOWELL**

In Warrensville, Ohio, Tonia Carmichael was still trying to pick up the pieces of the wreck she had made of her life. At forty-nine, she was a crack addict who had lost it all. Of course, to have lost it, you have to have had it, and relatively speaking, she had. At least for a while.

At the age of thirty-five, she had been a medical secretary and the owner of a three-bedroom brick home where she had been bringing up her three children as a single mother. But when she discovered drugs, things went south, fast. She quickly lost the house and the job. The kids went to live with her mother, Barbara Carmichael.

Not that Tonia's life had been entirely innocent until then. Tonia had always had troubles. She had her first daughter, Markiesha, when she was sixteen. Her second daughter, Donnita, was born two years later, in 1977, and son, Jonathan, was born in 1985. She never stuck with the fathers. Tonia had a string of criminal charges, starting in 1978 with grand theft, then a concealed weapons violation in 1982. In 1987, she was again charged with theft. Then she calmed down, got the house, the job. And she was an upstanding citizen, her mom, Barbara, said. She had some money, too; in 1996, Tonia joined some pals and hit the Las Vegas parties for the Mike Tyson–Evander Holyfield heavyweight title fight.

And at home, she was trying to keep her neighborhood safe.

"She was known for chasing drug dealers away," Barbara said.

But somehow along the line, Tonia began using the drugs instead of pushing them away. Once she lost everything, Tonia moved in with her kids and mom. The television and the car disappeared. She sold them for drug money. Her son's stereo went missing. One time, Tonia even tried to sell a camera to her daughter Donnita. Donnita refused.

In 2005, Tonia got popped on a drug charge and was sentenced to six months in the Ohio Reformatory for Women, in Marysville. It didn't do anything to deter her.

When she got out, she'd disappear for weeks, unexplained. When she came back, she'd sleep it off for a few days, then maybe get some temporary clerical work. Tonia still presented well, looked pretty good, and could do the job. But once she drew that first check, she'd be gone again. Sometimes she would turn her cell phone off, just so the people who loved her couldn't call and beg her to come back.

And Tonia's lifestyle was tinged with a bit of a death wish.

The way she was living, the five-feet-tall, 110-pound Tonia knew that her habits were putting her in danger. "You're going to miss me when I'm gone," she told her mother one day.

On the morning of November 10, 2008, Tonia asked her mother for $20 to buy antifreeze for her boyfriend's truck, a blue Chevy S-10 pickup, which she was borrowing. Barbara knew better. Since her daughter's relapse, she had been nickled and dimed by flimsy excuse after flimsy excuse. She remembered the car theft a few years back. But she couldn't refuse her daughter that day. She gave her the $20, and she watched Tonia drive away.

It was the last time she ever saw her. That night Barbara and the kids—now adults—went out in the cold autumn darkness and searched the area. Nothing.

"I called her for two days and nights, and I couldn't get her," Barbara said.

After the requisite forty-eight hours, Barbara and Markiesha walked into the Warrensville Heights Police Department to file a missing-persons report, but their report was met with indifference.

"She'll show up after she finishes smoking crack," Barbara said a desk sergeant told her.

The department, in a court document, said that Barbara and Markiesha, "purporting to be members" of Tonia Carmichael's family, "appeared at the Warrensville Heights Police Department inquiring about making a missing person's report and did not submit a report at that time."

As they continued to search the area for Tonia, they were told by some people in the neighborhood that she'd been seen around Imperial, about six miles away

Now Barbara went to the Fourth District station, which covers the Imperial area, to file a report. This time, she said, she was told that since Tonia wasn't a resident of the city of Cleveland, the office would not take a report. Cleveland police deny this.

A couple days later, Barbara found the pickup truck Tonia had been driving parked near the corner of 118th Street and Kinsman, about a ten-minute walk from the Sowell house on Imperial.

Barbara, sure that this evidence would prompt some help, went back to the Fourth District station and was again refused, but this time she was advised to file the report with the Warrensville Heights Police Department, and they would get the information there.

This time, Warrensville Heights took the report. Flyers were made and distributed. But like LeShanda Long, Tonia Carmichael had vanished.

Anthony Sowell was battling demons. He was losing Lori, and it hit him as hard as anything ever had.

"It's bad," he said later of that time beginning in 2008. "All the things I done, it's bad."

As his relationship with Lori Frazier moved to an end, he began to do anything he could to be part of her life.

Just before her arrest in early 2008, he went out with her on a night of drug cruising.

"I used to go out and hang with her. I just said 'what is so fascinating about this lifestyle?' I did it about three times, she would take me out where she hangs, abandoned buildings, trick houses . . . I spent the night in one where people hang out and get high but they—she make sure people there look after me."

"He's not a street dude," Lori told some of the people at the drug house. The houses were considered "safe" by users and sellers, hookers, and other small-time criminals in the Imperial area. Sowell did not typically frequent those places; he scored mostly from the locals on his block, and that was enough for him. Lori, though, had been in the street drug scene for years and knew the players.

"One dude was humongous, but he looked after me all night," Sowell said. "He wouldn't let . . . nothing happen. I just hung out with her and that morning I said I will be ready to go home."

When the time to get out came, Sowell turned to Lori.

"I don't see how you do it," he said.

Now, in the wake of their romance, Lori's visits were few. She still had more bags of clothes lying about, in spare rooms and in the basement, but she was too busy to deal with them. She was continuing to walk the straight line, trying to be a mother, trying to stay straight, visiting her community supervising officer, and working as many hours as she could at the restaurant downtown.

On Imperial, Sowell was keeping that front room on

the third floor locked down. And there seemed to be more jewelry and clothing about the house, more than was normal for a man who lived alone. He would have female guests in, but the collection of underwear, leggings, blouses, and shoes was growing.

There were leatherette coats with faux lamb's-wool collars, yellow thong underwear, underwear with purple psychedelic circles on it, Barbie underwear with pink lace at the top, chiffon panties—and all in different sizes. Sowell did little to hide the garments. He was a player now. This is what happened; his girls would leave things sometimes.

Gladys Wade would do anything for crack.

She started using at the age of twenty-four, in 1992, and stuck with it through the proverbial thick and thin. Crack was her faithful ally, for it stayed with her through her legal battles, a violence-spackled trail with charges of felonious assault and taking stolen property. She had been evicted, sued, and homeless at various times since that first taste of crack.

Gladys was a dedicated outlaw, repeatedly ignoring court summons and trial dates, then later getting picked up on open warrants. She was a hard-living, hard-fightin' woman who had grown up on mean streets and stayed there.

Before getting into the crack lifestyle, though, Gladys had graduated from Shaw High School in East

Cleveland—the same high school Anthony Sowell had attended a decade before her—where she was in the marching band. She then went to Central State University and enrolled in the music-education program.

"I was two classes short of graduating when I dropped out," Gladys says. "I ran out of money."

She had dabbled with drugs during college, but after she dropped out of Central, Gladys moved to Dayton, Ohio, with a boyfriend, "And that's when I got into drugs," she says.

The boyfriend fell away. The drugs didn't. She moved back to Cleveland and lived for a time with her mother, then her sister.

December 8, 2008, was a Monday, and Gladys was forty years old and two weeks out of the county jail after her latest encounter with the county's court system. The charge stemmed back to a severe beating of a maintenance man at her apartment building in May, for which both she and her live-in boyfriend, Thomas Leander, were arrested and indicted.

Both ignored the court date. Gladys was arrested shortly thereafter, but Thomas was still free, not exactly hiding out but lying low at their apartment in East Cleveland.

On that cold and gray December day, Gladys visited her sister, Twyla, who lived near Kinsman on the city's east side. She arrived in the afternoon and hung out for a while, just long enough for the two to get into a spat over some jeans Gladys had left there. She had other clothes at her sister's, and decided to take them with her to avoid any other problems. She stuffed them in a grocery bag and left the house around 5 P.M.

Gladys walked past the bus stop and kept moving toward the Imperial area, which was at the time a hotbed of drug activity. It was a thirty-minute walk, brisk in the thirty-five-degree air. She wanted a beer to take home, she said, and stopped at the market at the corner of 123rd and Imperial.

"I hadn't been there in years," Gladys said. She bought a twenty-four-ounce can of Labatt beer and a pack of cigarettes and stuck them in the bag with the clothes. It was dark out by now, and she headed west on Imperial toward 116th Street and the bus stop that would get her back to her place in East Cleveland.

As she crossed 123rd Street, Anthony Sowell walked up to her, astride, from the direction of the store. He was wearing a gray hoodie pulled up over his head and jeans and tennis shoes. There was a slight trace of snow on the ground, although a wintry slush was beginning to fall.

"Merry Christmas," she said, a little startled by his sidling.

"Merry Christmas," Sowell said. "Would you like to drink some beer tonight?"

Gladys didn't break stride as she uttered, "No thank you. I have my own."

Sowell fell back and watched.

Gladys walked on a bit more—ten seconds, perhaps—when she heard someone approaching, running.

Sowell pulled a powerful forearm across her throat, cutting off her air and rendering her unable to cry out. He pulled her quickly up the slight incline of the driveway as she twisted in his frenzied grip.

"I noticed the red house on the left, but I couldn't cry out because I was being choked," Gladys said. The house she was being taken into, she noticed, was the first house between the red house and Ray's Sausage, "the factory," as Gladys recalled it. A blue, older-model Chevrolet sedan blocked a clear path, but he hustled her past it and toward the side door, which led upstairs to his apartment.

Then everything went black. Sowell had choked her out with a strong-armed hold, and she was unconscious. He dragged her limp body up the stairs, through the small kitchenette, and down the narrow hallway to the sitting room at the front of the house. He turned on the lights to a small Christmas tree that sat in the corner at the front of the room.

Gladys awoke with a throbbing ache in her throat and a fast realization that she could die. She was in sheer terror. She screamed as loud as her injured vocal cords would allow. All it did was summon her attacker, Anthony Sowell. He ran into the room and, standing over her, punched her in the face several times with his fist.

"Bitch, take your clothes off," he bellowed.

At five feet seven and 150 pounds and with a hardened temper, Gladys Wade fought back the best way she could. From her angle on the floor, she knew how to disable a guy; she grabbed his balls.

"I did that, and I tried to take his arm off," she said.

"I was fighting back; he was fighting me. I ran to the stairs, and he's running after me."

The fight continued as she struggled to get to the stairs, any way she could. Gladys continued to call for help as best she was able.

"Bitch you can scream all you want, you're fixin' to die," Sowell said.

Although he had dragged her up the side-door steps, she pushed her way to the top of the front steps, which led to a door leading outside at the front of the house.

They fell down the wooden steps, Sowell on top of her, keeping his hands around her throat as tightly as he could.

They tumbled onto the landing on the second floor, and as they battled, Gladys's hand went through a glass plate in the top half of the door, severely lacerating her right thumb. Blood poured from the wound, and she kept pushing herself down the stairs as Sowell fought to drag her back up the stairs.

"Stop fighting!" he yelled, but she wouldn't stop. He told her repeatedly that she was going to die, and she would grab hold of his crotch and squeeze every chance she got.

It was wearing him down, and moving her up the stairs was proving to be too difficult. They fell once more down the second flight of stairs, and he gave up. He was severely cut himself now, as Gladys's nails had speared the skin around his eyes, and he had struck his head on a door frame, opening up a cut on the left side of his forehead.

She was free; she had escaped. Now she needed to get someone to make sure this guy would be locked up. The whole episode had happened so fast, within thirty minutes. It was now 6 P.M.

The full panic Gladys Wade had in her was uncontrollable, so when she ran into Bess Chicken and Pizza, the restaurant across the street from the Sowell house, it is not inconceivable that her babbling made her sound like one more crazy person in a neighborhood full of them. There were three customers in there, waiting for their food. They looked at her with disinterest.

"She came into my store, and she was really bleeding badly," says Fawcett Bess, who opened the place in 1990. He knew everyone in the area, but he had never seen Gladys before. And he was a little suspicious of her story.

"The blood was going all over the place, and she was crying. She was asking for someone to call the police. One of the customers told her there was a pay phone outside."

But the phone had long been disabled. Pay phones and drug neighborhoods don't mix.

Bess could make no sense of what Gladys was saying, but he told her she had to go outside, that blood and food can't be together. He grabbed a towel to wrap around her hand and called police from his cell phone, but as she stood there, Anthony Sowell walked across the street. In his hands, he held her jacket and sweater.

"He's telling [Bess] that 'the bitch stole my watch and stole my money,'" Gladys said. "They were laughing and saying all kinds of derogatory things like 'she was smoking crack and she robbed me.' They called him 'Tone.'"

She grabbed her jacket and began to run down 123rd Street and across a school yard to a house where her mother used to stay. She still knew the guys who lived there, and she used their phone to call her boyfriend.

It was a compromising situation for him; he had a warrant out for a serious felony. And if he did what he felt he should do—that is, administer some heavy street justice to Sowell—he would put himself at risk.

Gladys left the house and began to walk back toward the bus stop she had originally headed for before the nightmare. She was still bleeding, and her throat felt like broken glass. But she was still running and looking, fearing that Sowell was looking for her to finish the job.

"I still didn't know if he was coming after me," she said. "I just kept running and found some police."

Cleveland Police Department officer Kevin Walker was assigned to Fourth District patrol that evening, working the second shift, 3:30 P.M. to 1:30 A.M. Walker was a twelve-year veteran of the department, a barrel-chested, bald-headed cop with a mustache, a central-casting law-enforcement guy who had spent all of his years in this high-crime district. Before coming to the department, he'd been a juvenile-detention officer for five years.

As Walker and his patrol partner, Angel Serra, sat at a stoplight on southbound 116th Street, they saw Gladys Wade, waving her arms. It was around 6:30 P.M. She was bleeding badly from her hand, and Walker saw that she had a towel and napkins around the wound. It was a pretty bad cut, he thought. He called for an ambulance, and between his assessment of her injury and his calling for help, Gladys told them her story.

"She said there was an attempted rape by a man that she knows, 'Tone,' or she said she knew of him," Walker said. "She said she heard people from the neighborhood call him that."

Gladys faithfully relayed information that checked out—a dark sedan in the driveway, signs of a struggle in the snow near the house, her blood on the walls and stairs. And she described Anthony Sowell—that he was wearing a gray hoodie, a black skullcap with white lettering on it, and jeans, and that he was real skinny and had a dark complexion, with spare facial hair. He should also have some scratches on his face, she said.

"If you go over there now, he should be there," she told them. Then she added, "I kicked his butt."

Another police unit arrived to stay with her, and Walker and Serra headed over to 12205 Imperial.

They arrived to a scene that had been faithfully rendered by Gladys. Car in driveway, dark sedan. Signs of a struggle in the disturbed snow outside the side door. Blood on the stairway and the walls of the stairwell. Broken glass on the second-floor landing. They called for backup, but before the car arrived, Sowell poked his head out of the third-floor apartment and looked at the officers on the landing. He hadn't even changed his clothes.

"What's going on?" he asked the officers, who by now had their weapons drawn. It was the reported scene of a crime, after all. They ordered him down the stairs, slowly.

Sowell was read his rights and cuffed. And, just as Gladys had said, he had some scratches on his face as well as two big cuts, including one that was coming up as a knot on his head.

Gladys was taken by ambulance to University Hospital, where she was treated by Renee Hotz, a sexual-assault nurse. Hotz clipped Gladys's nails and swabbed her hands for DNA evidence. Gladys was joined at the hospital by Thomas Leander, who took her home.

The next day, Gladys met with Cleveland Police Detective Georgia Hussein, part of the department's sex crimes unit. Hussein saw the injuries, no doubt; her hand required stitches and the police report noted that she had "several red scratches on her neck" when the cops first saw her. But there hadn't been any sexual assault; as Gladys told Hussein, "He tried to kill me."

"I'm not sure why I was talking to [Hussein]," Gladys said. Once she told her that there was no rape, Hussein "told me who [Sowell] was . . . she told me his record."

Indeed, police routinely check the sex-offender registry when someone is accused of a sexual assault, as police first believed was the case here. An alleged rape case automatically goes to the sex crimes unit.

Gladys also told police, as an aside, that she'd had $11 in cash in the pocket of her jacket, which was held as evidence, and that Sowell had taken her can of beer and unopened pack of cigarettes.

Gladys was released after meeting with Hussein and came back the next day to the department headquarters to sign a paper giving detectives access to her medical records from the night before and give a written statement.

At the city jail, investigators photographed Sowell's injuries, and he was put in a cell. In addition to the scratches and gouges on his face and head, he had scrapes on his legs and shoulders. It had been one helluva fight.

Detectives fanned out in the small section of Imperial and quizzed witnesses. Fawcett Bess, the patrons of his restaurant, and a couple neighbors were all questioned.

The next day, December 10, 2008, Cleveland Police Department detectives met with Assistant City Prosecutor Lorrain Coyne. The consensus was that there was insufficient evidence of a crime to prosecute.

According to an investigative report police did not see any "visible signs" of Gladys Wade having been punched in the face.

Hours after that report was turned in, around 6 P.M., Sowell was let go on something called a "straight release." It was a practice that had been in place for years in Cleveland, brought about because of crowding at the city jail. Straight release gave investigators twenty-four to forty-eight hours to assemble the needed facts to make a case and put the accused before the city's municipal court for bond requirements and a preliminary hearing to move prosecution forward.

According to the notes of Cleveland prosecutor Victor Perez, the case was dropped in part because the "detective did not believe the victim was credible."

Although straight release was a practical approach to the crowding problem, as well as an overburdened courts system, it sometimes resulted in an investigation that was not as complete as it might be. Ideally, a case might stay on the radar even after a straight release and a more solid case was built for an indictment. But in practice, dangerous criminals were sometimes let go.

Gladys, who had been pressing the department for information, was dumbstruck. She had never heard of straight release.

Anthony Sowell grabbed a bus back to the house on Imperial, where he cleaned up the mess left from the fracas with Gladys. It was almost Christmas. He went over to the store and got some beer.

# CHAPTER 9

You could be the next crackhead bitch dead in the street.

**—ANTHONY SOWELL**

"After my girl and me broke up, I just . . . [it was] traumatic, very traumatic," Anthony Sowell said, a couple of years after Lori Frazier left him.

He was indeed having a hard time, going into dreamlike states where he would thrash around, violently, screaming, tearing at people, whoever was there in this blur. And when he would come out from this state, he would appear "just like everything is ok," he said.

By then, at the start of 2009, the voices he claimed he had heard shortly after Lori left became louder.

"I couldn't tell them no," he said. "It's like hate, punish, hot."

Sowell was now living alone in the house. Segerna left for good in early 2009 as she began dialysis treatment. She moved in with her mother, Virginia Oliver, and Sowell would go visit her almost every week. The first floor on Imperial was left in the same spotless condition she had always kept it.

Jermaine, Segerna's nephew, continued to come by several times a week to check on the place, crash, and sometimes party.

Sowell mostly left the second floor alone. The main living room—like on the third floor, the room sat to the front of the house overlooking Imperial—had a lone blue upholstered chair and a grab bag of CDs, including titles by Ray Charles, Mariah Carey, and Jay-Z.

But the third floor was a disaster area.

Empty glasses and cups sat on tables and dressers in his room, where Sowell now spent much of his time. It was the same room he and Lori shared, on the east side of the house. There was a good-sized double window in it that opened onto a narrow alley between the house and Ray's Sausage.

The mattress and box spring had fallen off the bed frame, and now the headboard leaned nonchalantly and unattached against the wall. He hung baseball caps on the two posts of the headboard, and he stacked his medications on the boom box that sat on the nightstand next to the bed. On a wooden five-drawer dresser, the kind grandmas everywhere seemed to hand down to kids, Sowell kept his TV, which was connected to a Game Boy. And next to that, he stacked stereo gear; from the bottom up, a solid state amplifier, a cassette deck, and a turntable.

Pornographic magazines, the kind that come wrapped in plastic at three for $6.99, with titles like *Tender* and

*Barely Legal,* lay on coffee tables, while skin flicks jostled
with Hollywood titles in makeshift DVD racks. His
clothes were strewn in piles around the room, dirty sweat-
shirts and jeans with boots and sneakers haphazardly
tossed about.

The kitchen, at the south end of the hall and opening
onto the back stairway, was also a mess, with dirty dishes
and take-out food containers joining empty beer bottles
and cans on the narrow counter.

Where he'd once been orderly and neat, a trait he'd
learned in the military, now Sowell's third-floor apartment
on Imperial was strewn with garbage and the detritus of
a man falling apart.

An hour was like a day, a day like a month, as Donald
Smith waited for his daughter Kim Y. Smith to return
home. She had left his apartment on January 17, 2009,
to go out for the night. Where was she, two days later?

The wheelchair-bound Donald was planning a party
for Kim's forty-fourth birthday on the next day, January
20. She wouldn't miss that for the world, he thought.

Donald was a Marine Corps veteran who doted on
Kim, who, by the start of 2009, was his de facto personal
assistant as well as his loving daughter. She cooked and
cleaned for him, making sure he had everything he needed
in his apartment near the fashionable Shaker Square area
of Cleveland. Kim was an angel to her father, a little less
so to the rest of society, although she had tried to make
good. She graduated from Warrensville Heights High

School and took some classes at the local community college, mostly art and dance.

But as she acquired a drug problem, Kim preferred to hang out in bad places. Her street name was Candy, and she was frequently seen in the Imperial area, walking around, looking for drugs, partying with friends. Six of her eleven county court cases were crack-related—possessing it or using it. The rest were for more advanced crimes, things like receiving stolen property and extortion.

Donald figured she had picked up a drug habit her last year of high school, where she ran with an older, faster crowd. He had lost touch with her in that time, but when he discovered her affliction, he moved to remedy it.

"I had taken her to several clinics in and out of Ohio," Donald said. She was getting locked up in prison for her out-of-control drug problem, and Donald had hoped there would be some relief for her there, maybe some treatment or counseling.

"In some of the institutions she was in, she got drugs inside the institutions," he said, flustered and saddened. His daughter was determined to be suicidal by the courts, and she was placed in mental-health-evaluation clinics. She took antidepressants. She committed more crimes. In 2004, she was again caught with drugs.

At the end of 2007, Kim got out of prison after serving a six-month sentence for drugs. She moved back in with her father, but it didn't take long before she was taking off and not coming home for days.

But January 17, 2009, the last day he'd seen her, had

been a good day. Donald had handed his daughter $100 before she went shopping with her aunt. He loved her, and she knew it, he was sure. He'd encouraged her to get anything she wanted.

Kim scored some clothes, went to lunch. Later, she kissed her father before she headed out for the night.

After two days, Donald contacted her friends and put together a flyer with a picture of Kim. Being a man of relative means, Donald sweetened the pot with a $500 reward.

"On the street, $500 is like a million," he said.

He never contacted the Cleveland Police Department. It just wasn't always the first place people went for help when there was trouble in the bad areas of town.


How many times had Amelda Hunter been to Anthony Sowell's house? She couldn't even count. She'd see her friends around, and sometimes they'd all end up at Tone's, drinking and smoking and carrying on.

The house at 12205 Imperial was a gathering place for the addicted, the disenfranchised, and the criminal. And Amelda had battled back and forth with that lifestyle. Yet she was also a mom of two kids and a life mate to Bobby Dancy. There was some hope at the end of a pretty rough forty-seven years. She had a decent home, a pleasant 1,100-square-foot, two-bed, one-bath number, in a decent neighborhood a few blocks east and a whole world away from Imperial. Her other home-away-from-home, though, was a rancid room in a house on Imperial and, more and more frequently, Sowell's place.

Amelda was born in 1962 in Chicago, the sixth of eight children, where she was brought up on the city's crime-riddled South Side. She was impregnated by a teacher at her school when she was fourteen. That had jolted her family and spurred a move to her mother's native Cleveland two years later, in 1978. But instead of helping, things just got worse from there. Most of the kids in the family, the ones left at home, got turned on to drugs, first relatively minor things like weed and drink, but when crack came along in the mid-1980s, they joined in with gusto.

Amelda was no exception. Her older sister Lynnette abetted in the delinquency of her younger sisters. She would take Amelda and some of the others to bars in the city's sordid areas, exposing them to all kinds of the wrong things that would tempt a teenager.

"They were too young to be in those places, but as long as they didn't tell my mother, we would go," Lynnette said. "They grew up fast, messing with me."

In fact, Amelda met Bobby Dancy in a Cleveland bar in 1981. He was a machine operator, a hard-drinking, blue-collar man who didn't mess with drugs. She was still hooked on crack, although she was a smart user; he didn't know for years that she was an addict.

She went for years without a serious drug case, in fact. After a fifteen-year stretch in which she had very little contact with the law, Amelda was busted in 2001 for possession of drugs, got some prison time, then went into rehab. She was off paper, or out of the control of the state, in May 2004.

By March 2005, she was back in court for another drug-possession charge. She was released with time served, a couple of weeks.

She went home to Bobby's house on Imperial, but even he knew that the area was getting too bad to stay there with Amelda, who would now sometimes be gone for weeks at a time without calling.

So in 2006, they left Imperial and moved a few blocks east.

Still, Amelda kept going back to the old neighborhood. And now she had a new pal, Anthony Sowell.

One evening in late 2007, Denise Hunter joined her sister for a night out. They walked a few blocks away to 12205, and Denise recalled walking in and seeing several women sitting around, talking. Someone offered the Hunter sisters something to drink.

Denise was creeped out, especially by the familiarity her sister had with this crew.

"I got the impression she had seen the ladies before," Denise said. "It was like, 'Come on in; have a seat.' "

Older sister Lynnette Hunter Taylor said when Amelda would disappear in 2007, more and more frequently she'd head for 12205.

"When she would leave and be gone for a little while, that's whose house she was at," Lynnette said. "The impression she gave me of Anthony Sowell was this was a nice man, that he was nice to her and did whatever he could for her. He was her buddy."

The last time Amelda was seen, on April 18, 2009, her son, Bobbie, says, "She took off walking because she didn't have a car. And she had a hurt left arm from something, so she was somewhat immobilized."

When she didn't come back by the evening, something wasn't right, he says.

"We were supposed to go to my aunt's, and it just didn't seem at this time that she would pull this kind of thing, even though she had disappeared for weeks at a time before."

He walked over to the Imperial area, knowing that his mom still crashed at Bobby Dancy's old house on Imperial, which was now vacant.

He stopped at the take-out place across from Anthony Sowell's place on 12205 Imperial, Bess Chicken and Pizza, and talked to Fawcett Bess, the owner.

"He said he had seen her over across the street," Bobbie says. "But he didn't know exactly when."

Bobbie didn't report her missing, though, instead embarking on his own search, like Donald Smith had for his daughter Kim. Bobbie was joined by Denise and the rest of the family, who put out posters everywhere in the neighborhood.

Nothing.

With the parade of drug-using women going in and out of 12205, it was hard to tell who was there and when. "All of those girls were around there, and they all came into my store," says Sam Tayeh. They bought him out of Chore Boy, steel wool used as a filter when smoking crack, and lighters, sometimes a dozen at a time.

Anthony Sowell arrives in court for a hearing shortly after his arrest in October 2009.

JOHN KUNTZ/*THE PLAIN DEALER*/ LANDOV

ABOVE: The house at 12205 Imperial, where Sowell took the lives of eleven women (front view).

RIGHT: (back view)

CUYAHOGA COUNTY CORONER'S OFFICE

Nancy Cobbs
CUYAHOGA COUNTY SHERIFF'S OFFICE

LeShanda Long
CUYAHOGA COUNTY SHERIFF'S OFFICE

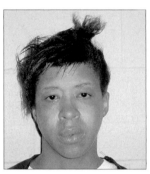

Kim Yvette Smith
CUYAHOGA COUNTY SHERIFF'S OFFICE

Tonia Carmichael
CUYAHOGA COUNTY COURT
OF COMMON PLEAS

Janice Webb
CUYAHOGA COUNTY SHERIFF'S OFFICE

Diane Turner
CUYAHOGA COUNTY SHERIFF'S OFFICE

Crystal Dozier

Amelda Hunter

Tishana Culver

Telacia Fortson

Lori Frazier, Anthony Sowell's girlfriend

Workers from the coroner's office pulling up a bagged body buried by Sowell in his backyard.

Most of the graves Sowell dug in the backyard were less than twenty-four inches deep.

LEFT: Officers executing the warrant to arrest Sowell for rape in October 2009 found disturbed dirt beneath the basement stairs. The body of Janice Webb was found buried under a foot of earth.

BELOW: Crawl space in the third floor sitting room at the house on Imperial, where the remains of Tishana Culver were found.

An officer checks the walls in the hallway next to the sitting room on the third floor. After finding Tishana Culver's body in a crawl space, searchers tore through the walls looking for other hidden bodies.

Members of the Cuyahoga County coroner's office study the ceiling in the kitchen of 12205 Imperial as they search for more bodies.

Anthony Sowell's bedroom in his third floor apartment.

Receipts, jewelry, pill bottles, and a bus pass were among the evidence seized at the Imperial house.

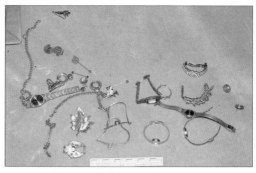

Search teams found jewelry from almost
every victim at the house.

A number of ligatures and strangling tools were discovered
both on the victims and around the house.

Victims' phones were also found around the house,
their batteries removed.

Imperial Beverage, three doors down from 12205 Imperial, was frequented by Sowell, as well as most of his victims.   DANIEL OWEN

In the days following the discovery of the bodies, community members posted pictures and descriptions of their missing loved ones, wondering who else might be among Sowell's victims.   DANIEL OWEN

\*    \*    \*

Tanja Doss, who had dated Anthony Sowell before he got together with Lori Frazier, had vowed to get her boyfriend back, and now was her chance. But like so many girls on the street in the Imperial area, she was dancing with an addiction much more heartily than she was pursuing romance.

In the spring of 2007, Tanja had returned to Cleveland from New York, where she was caring for her stroke-stricken mother. She lived in the area, scoring from the numerous area dealers. Back then, Sowell was taken; now, he was available.

Like almost everyone on the block, Tanja had several criminal convictions, and she had done six months in the Ohio Reformatory for Women for violating her probation sentence in a drug-possession case. She had various other infractions, from domestic violence to theft. She was another raspy voiced, fortysomething street girl in a neighborhood full of them.

Over the years—Tanja and Sowell had known each other since 2005, when Sowell was fresh out of prison. They would talk about their respective pasts, though he never copped to his rape charge, and Tanja never asked.

In fact, Sowell's sexual-offender status was not common knowledge on the street. And despite his ebbing health and his emaciated state, Tone was still known as a good guy who could change out your water heater and rewire your electricity.

"I don't know about you, but I never committed any

crime," he told Tanja when they first got together in 2005. "I took a manslaughter rap for my brother."

And that was the last they ever talked about his decade-and-a-half imprisonment. It was commonly believed among the folks that gathered at his house that the cops would stick a black man in jail and it often didn't matter who'd done what.

Tanja ran into him in mid-April 2009 as he walked back from a store on 116th Street clutching a bag of beer; it was past 10 P.M., and the store on Imperial was closed. They were happy to see each other.

"Hey T, come on by some time," Sowell said, calling her by the name he knew best. They exchanged cell-phone numbers.

"I had heard they broke up," Tanja said, regarding Anthony and Lori. "And that's all he ever talked about, and he said she was coming back, and he had clothes of hers, and he was going to get those to her." Still, a few days after running into each other on the street, she came over and they slept together for the first time since 2005. It was familiar and easy. She didn't get high, nor did he.

She said she'd noticed Sowell's physical decline when she saw him around the neighborhood when she got back.

"He had started losing weight and not looking the same," she said. "I assumed that he was smoking because of the weight loss, and he was thinner, and he wasn't dressing like he used to. He was a good dresser in 2005, and now when I started seeing him, he was raggedy, not Tony to me."

Again, he invited her over, this time with the promise

of drugs and beer. He was up front—he said he was getting paid so he'd take care of the party favors, and she could spend the night.

Tanja's best friend, Nancy Cobbs, was spending time at Sowell's as well, although their relationship was more a function of necessity; Cobbs's boyfriend was selling Sowell crack. Nancy turned forty-three on April 20, and she and Tanja scored some drugs and celebrated.

"I'm going to Tony's tomorrow night," Tanja told her. "You should come with me."

It was a plan, but when the next afternoon arrived, Nancy decided to go to her boyfriend's place instead. So Tanja called Sowell and told him she'd come over by herself. It was around four in the afternoon, a dismal, cold, rainy day, when she walked from her place on Forest over to Imperial. A cousin of hers was staying across the street from the Sowell house, and she spent a little time there, but around 8 P.M., she headed over to Sowell's. It was, again, a welcome visit for her, because she truly liked him.

Sowell already had a few rocks and some beer ready to go, so they began that easy chatter that was made looser by the beer. The two had some beers and smoked a bit, watching the Cavs beat the Detroit Pistons in game 2 of the NBA play-offs.

"We started smoking, then looking at the game, cheering," Tanja said. "After we watched the game, we started listening to music and talking about different things. He talked about how he was missing his girlfriend."

The two were having a nice time. Tanja was remembering why she always liked to see him. It was warm with him.

Then he asked why she hadn't called him the previous week, after they had been together.

Sowell had set up the dresser for his pipe, his wire, and his lighters.

As he asked her about her failure to call him, Sowell was standing with his back turned to Tanja, who was sitting on the side of the twin bed near the end.

He was clearing the pipe to smoke some more. She was looking away, toward the window while he was to her left and behind her.

Then he sprung.

Within seconds, Sowell had Tanja—his friend, his lover—by the throat and was pushing her up the mattress toward the disconnected headboard that leaned against the wall. At five feet four and 81 pounds, the diminished, intoxicated woman had no chance to even fight back.

Tears began to flow involuntarily as she gasped for breath and looked into Sowell's enraged face, which had transformed almost instantly, like a science-fiction movie monster who could switch physical and emotional appearances at will. It was a haywire Jekyll-Hyde conversion.

"Bitch, you could be the next crackhead bitch dead in the street and nobody would give a fuck about you," he roared into her face. The music continued to play, but the violence of his attack and the rapid cutoff of oxygen made it sound distant and surreal. His thumbs dug deeply into each side of her neck, closing off her jugular veins.

He had pushed her onto her back, her arms outstretched at the head of the mattress.

"If you want to live, knock three times on the floor," he commanded her.

Tanja used the side of her left hand—*bam, bam, bam*—pounding the wooden floor. He pulled his hands away and stood up. Tanja sat up on the edge of the bed.

"Tony, why you trippin' like that?" she asked peering up. Tears, now from her distraught emotional state as well as from the choking, were flowing down her cheeks.

He reached down and slapped her in the face, hard.

"Bitch, shut the fuck up and take off your clothes," he said. His face was twisted into the mask of a madman.

She obeyed him, and as she did so, she felt her face swelling from the slaps.

"Move, Tony, let me go to the bathroom and see my face," Tanja said. She was scared, but there was still the element of familiarity she felt with him. She had been abused by men before, even raped, so talking to her friend turned tormentor still seemed easy.

She took a left out the bedroom door and walked to the bathroom to check on her face. And when she returned to the bedroom, Sowell was sprawled, naked on his back, hands behind his head in repose.

"Tony, why you trippin' like this?" she said again, beseeching him.

"I should make you suck my dick," he said to her, his voice harsh and stern, like a drill sergeant.

Still standing, she leaned down and picked up her pants, hoping to get dressed and get away. She pondered her escape routes. The window behind her, although it was three stories up, would land her on the empty driveway. It was painted shut and she would have to break through the glass.

"Bitch, who told you to put your clothes on?" he demanded.

She dropped her pants back to the floor and crawled timidly onto the bed, curling into a fetal position, being as small as she could.

"I was praying and I cried myself to sleep," Tanja said. She was exhausted and terrified and scared straight. She had no idea what time it was.

When she awoke, it was 11 A.M. and the skies were still a deep gray, and a cold wind blew the rain that was falling.

Sowell got up and looked at her like nothing had ever happened, as if the maniac that he had become was no longer home.

"You want a beer or something?" he asked.

"No, I just want a pop, if you got it," Tanja answered, hoping, praying that it wouldn't bring more abuse.

Tony was back, and whoever that was who took over eight hours ago was gone, as if he'd forgotten the whole thing.

Tanja had not. She'd fallen asleep scared and woke up scared. She had to get out before the whole thing started again. Her daughter Tashana had just had a baby. That was her out.

"I made up a story about her baby being sick and I had to go to the hospital," she said. She placed a fake phone call to Tashana, not really dialing the phone. She said into the phone that she was on her way.

Tanja dressed and walked down the front stairway, with Sowell joining her.

"Let me know that she's okay, call me," he said as they parted at the sidewalk in front of the house. Tanja went right, and he went left. She wouldn't see him again for a couple of years.

Tanja never told the police. She had seen plenty of crime and taken part in some. And besides, she thought, in the end he just slapped her and choked her. What would the police do for a spat between crackheads?

But she did tell Nancy Cobbs, her best friend.

"He went crazy and choked the shit outta me" is how Tanja described it to Nancy. The two had met in kindergarten and had shared plenty of secrets and gossip over their more than thirty-five-year friendship. Later, Tanja would also tell Janice Webb, another friend from around the neighborhood who knew Anthony Sowell. Both were surprised; certainly that wasn't the guy they knew.

# CHAPTER 10

I'm sorry. I thought you were my daughter.
She's been missing for a while.
**—ADLEAN ATTERBERRY**

When the penal system turned him loose in 2005, the state authorities had determined that Anthony Sowell had a minimal possibility of reoffending.

There are mounds of paper amid mountains of studies on recidivism for sexual offenders. Some people believe that if there is even the remotest chance of again committing a deviant crime, why let them out at all?

Sowell was released under Megan's Law, which merely required an annual reporting by Sowell to the Cuyahoga County Sheriff's Office, which he did. A deputy from the office stopped by the house periodically to verify that Sowell was still there.

He was not on parole or probation, but he was fully registered as a sex offender at his address. The system of registration is managed by the county sheriff's office. Not the Cleveland Police Department, which investigated

Gladys Wade's allegations. And just because Wade talked with the city police department's sex crimes unit didn't mean that they would confer with the sheriff's office.

And Sowell was not creating big problems for the cops in his neighborhood in the early part of 2009, even though the sex crimes unit had obviously been aware of some street chatter; after all, a Cleveland Police Department detective mentioned it to Wade as she interviewed her.

Nancy Cobbs liked Anthony Sowell, even after hearing from her best friend, Tanja Doss, about the weird freakout he had that April night. Maybe he was just too high.

Nancy had been staying with Audrey Williams, her twenty-two-year-old daughter, in public housing on Quincy Avenue, about three miles from Imperial. She'd been there for about six weeks, still trying to find out what she was going to do with herself.

Nancy had just turned forty-three years old, and she was again trying a comeback. She was born in Cleveland in 1966 and dropped out of high school after she got pregnant, at fifteen. Nancy married the father, William Hunt, who soon joined the military and left to serve his hitch. They had a son, William III, and divorced.

In the mid-1980s, Nancy made a couple moves that changed her life. First, she met Adam Williams at a nightclub. He was a good man, and they stuck together for almost a decade. They liked to party together, but when Nancy got pregnant with their daughter, Audrey, Adam decided it was time to get serious about having a family. But Nancy couldn't stop the party life, and when Adam left for Wichita, Kansas, to attend truck-driving school to learn a trade, Nancy decided to stay in her native Cleveland. The next year, 1995, Nancy was caught in a large bust for drug trafficking. It was a hard case; Nancy and five others were sent up, with Nancy getting a three- to fifteen-year sentence. The kids went to live with her mom, Louvenia.

She served two years, then got paroled in 1998.

When Nancy got out, she picked up right where she'd left off. Within eighteen months, she was popped again for possessing crack and was sent back to prison.

Her daughter, Audrey, would visit her at the prison, bitter over how things had turned out but still tied to her mom through a love that seemed to have no bounds. It was the drug habit she just didn't get.

"I never approved of it, and we used to get into fights because I wanted to see her better herself," Audrey said. "After my mother and father separated, she just would be in the streets."

By 2008, Nancy was hanging out with this guy in the neighborhood whom everyone cheerfully called "Tone."

Nancy, Tanja, Amelda—they all knew him. He would come by once in a while and sit on the porch at Nancy's house, a few blocks from Imperial, and drink beer with them. Audrey didn't care, of course. It was harmless, and Sowell seemed benign. She'd say hi to him when he was there.

So on April 24, 2009, when Nancy spent the day at

the house on Quincy before announcing that she had plans for the evening, it drew a weary sigh from the kids.

"She had just got her hair cut short," Audrey remembered. "She told me she and her friend were going somewhere with Tanja Doss."

Nancy left the house around 5 P.M. Later that evening, Nancy called Audrey, mentioning that she was with someone and that everything was okay. But after Audrey hung up, something didn't seem right. She just couldn't figure out what it was. But Nancy didn't come home that night. Calls to her cell phone went unanswered for the next few days. Then it became a week, and she missed a May 1 doctor's appointment.

"They called to see if she was coming," said Kyana, another of Nancy's daughters, "and I called her phone and didn't get anyone. That was my first sign. I started calling her friends and no one could find her. Mom would go away but never to a point where we couldn't get in touch with her. Never like she went away and [we] couldn't talk to her."

Audrey Williams went to the Cuyahoga Metropolitan Housing Authority Police Department to file a missing-persons report. She was directed to the Cleveland Police Department Fourth District station. But instead of filing a report, Audrey and the rest of the family and their friends, including Tanja Doss, went out on May 9, plastering the neighborhoods with flyers that read:

Nancy Cobbs (43): Missing Since 4/29/09, from Cleveland, Ohio. DOB: 4/20/66; female, 5'3", 125 lbs, Race-black, Hair-black, short; Eyes-brown. Nancy was last seen after she left her house to go to a store on East 116 near Continental. The last time she spoke to her daughter was around 5 pm that day. She was wearing blue jean capris, a white blouse, a short black leather jacket, and New Balance shoes.

They talked a local TV station, WEWS, the ABC affiliate, into graciously running an item on its website.

*A local family is spending Mother's Day without their mom. Now they are taking action and turning to the community for help to find her. Nancy Cobbs left her home on April 24 to go to a neighborhood store and that was the last time anyone saw the Cleveland mother. On Saturday, family, friends and neighbors desperate to find her held an emotional rally for the 43-year-old Cobbs. "I know something was wrong because she didn't answer her phone. Her phone has been going straight to voice mail and that's not like my mother," her daughter said. "I don't want to think it's foul play, I really don't. I'm hoping she might be somewhere and just hasn't called." Cobbs is the mother of three children and many grandchildren who are heartbroken over her disappearance. She is 5 feet 3 inches, 125 pounds and was last seen wearing blue jean capris, a white blouse and black leather jacket. Cobbs' family said the greatest gift would be a reunion with their mom on Mother's Day. Her family said Cobbs was healthy and had no medical issues.*

The segment ended with a plea that anyone with any information on her disappearance contact the Cleveland Police Department Fourth District station, but nothing came of it.

Nancy Cobbs joined the growing number of women missing from the streets around Imperial.

The many missing-person posters that had been slapped up on any surface—telephone poles, store windows, and any of the many flat, blank spaces in the Imperial area—were being torn down.

Families and friends would traverse the area, even extending beyond the immediate eight to ten blocks around Imperial, with staple guns, glue, and tape, hoping that just one of the crudely designed flyers would yield a lead. Some simply wanted to know the morbid answer: alive or dead? Others were simply hoping a tipster would give a call and let them know that the missing was holed up somewhere and would be home eventually.

"We put posters . . . in the surrounding area, and the next day, when we'd ride by, they were all gone," Adlean Atterberry, the mother of the missing Michelle Mason, said.

One day in late spring 2009, Adlean had been driving through the Imperial area. Her daughter, Michelle Mason, never left her mind even though she had been gone since October. As she waited at a stoplight, she looked over to her right and spotted a woman who, at a glance, looked like Michelle. She pulled her car to the curb and rolled down the window for a closer look. But it wasn't Michelle.

"I'm sorry. I thought you were my daughter. She's been missing for a while," she told the woman. And she drove on. Hope springs eternal, always.

Employees at Imperial Beverage told her that whenever Sowell came in, the posters would be gone when he left. "Flyers were gone from some of the areas . . . they were gone, too," she said.

"My family did the same thing," Florence Bray, Crystal Dozier's mom, added. "We put posters on the east side and west side."

They would be torn down as soon as they were put up.

On the first Wednesday in June 2009, Telacia Fortson walked into her mom's kitchen, her arms loaded down by five bags full of groceries, including some chicken, which she fried up as soon as everything else was put away.

Then she cleaned the place, up and down, top to bottom. It was always a clean house anyway, a place full of chimes and plants and an aura of gentle nature. A white picket fence encased a small yard that was graced by a porcelain angel surrounded by porcelain doves. It was a house kissed with love in a neighborhood that had fallen down over the years. The neat, two-story house stood like a beacon to better years, as if by just existing it could summon a better day.

Telacia loved Inez Fortson, the woman who had

adopted her when she was nine years old. Inez was a divorced woman living alone when she adopted Telacia, who had been in the Cuyahoga County's foster-care system for four years. Her birth mother was a drug addict, and her daddy was a drunk. Neither was fit to care for a child. But Telacia hadn't always been a model daughter to Inez.

Now thirty-one, she had been in trouble since she was a juvenile, starting with smoking pot at the age of fourteen and graduating to cocaine at twenty. As a teenager, she'd run away from Inez and her world of beauty, instead seeking what she considered freedom, which served as a convenient mask for delinquency.

She would often run to a former foster mother, Lucille Groomster, who lived four miles away.

"She would always run to my grandmother," said Ebony Groomster, thirty-six, Lucille's granddaughter. "My grandmother never closed the door on her, no matter what the repercussions were."

In fact, despite the cushy life Inez provided, Telacia had bounced around town as a teenager, staying with other friends as well as Lucile Groomster.

Inez would try to exert some discipline, but it didn't work, and she didn't have the will for a fight.

Inevitably, at seventeen years old, Telacia ended up at Bellefaire JCB, a residential facility for wayward youth. The place offered help for drug problems, behavior issues, mental-health troubles. It was a catchall for juveniles. And Telacia wasn't having any of the help, getting in fights and damaging property. In 1997, having completed high school classes, she was evicted from Bellefaire in a complaint filed by the facility in June.

She hit the streets for a life of crime and drugs. She was sent by the court for mental-health treatment. She had suicide attempts behind her. She had anger issues. She was popped for drug possession a couple of times; then, in 2003, while under court supervision, she tested positive for cocaine while she was pregnant with her first child. She didn't know who the father was. The child was delivered, and the county took custody of the child.

"Mother has engaged in acts of domestic violence; child at risk," a social worker's report stated. "Mother has attempted suicide on four occasions."

Telacia also washed out of three drug-treatment programs and was living on the streets or with a boyfriend, Terrance Minor, who had a rap sheet longer than hers, with several violent offenses.

"Does not have a permanent home," the social worker duly noted, adding, "Lacks the parenting skills to care for the child. Has only visited sporadically."

By 2006, Telacia had two kids—neither of whom she had custody of—and was pregnant by Minor. She was twenty-eight and checked into Laura's Home, a shelter for women run by the City Mission. She sang in the shelter's choir, took some job training, and headed back into the world in early 2007. She failed and came back a few months later. Telacia cried as she told staffers at the home about her situation. She told one that if she were to go back out to the streets, she was sure she would end up dead.

"I know I can get some peace here," she told the shelter staffers. Yet Telacia walked away the next day.

In 2008 came the theft rap and the prison time. While locked up, she sent a friend a letter about how she let Inez Fortson down.

"I feel like an outcast in her family. But as I continued to pray to the Lord, it has gotten a little better each day, knowing that it is only one more day closer to me being a productive citizen and a good mom to my children."

She got out, became reacquainted with Inez, and hit the streets again, only this time she had a Bible in one hand and a crack pipe in the other.

Terrance Minor had custody of two of her three children when she got out, and she stayed at his house frequently. He had gone relatively straight: no felonies since 2001.

Telacia went into Imperial Beverage with a friend from a local church; her new life was based on faith, she told people. She bought a soda instead of a beer.

But when she disappeared, it was after another visit to the store. That time, she'd bought four lighters.

A while passed before Inez became worried. She thought her daughter was on the straight and narrow, so where was she?

She called the East Cleveland Police Department, which sent a car to her house to take a report. The officers provided her with a list of morgues, hospitals, and other police departments and law-enforcement agencies around the city. She called them diligently, but no one had a thing on Telacia. She and her lighters had disappeared.

*  *  *

Janice Webb could have been voted most likely to go missing.

At forty-eight years old, she would frequently walk the streets of the Imperial neighborhood, looking to score some crack. And when she did, she made no secret of it—she would buy a dozen lighters at a time at Imperial Beverage, and throw in a box of Chore Boy, the steel wool that worked so nicely as a filter in crack paraphernalia.

Other than some traffic stops and fines, Janice had managed to avoid serious trouble with the law since 2003, when she had been busted for possession of crack along with some friends.

But Janice was a model defendant in the case. She was bonded out after her arrest in July of that year, and she showed up for every court appearance, unlike most of her peers. And she caught a break, at first probation, drug treatment, frequent drug testing, and mandatory sobriety for a year.

She walked out of court a week before Christmas, but within two months, in February 2004, she tested positive for cocaine and was back before the judge. House detention, the judge said this time. Another break.

But by April, Janice was gone, no longer reporting to the required Alcoholics Anonymous meetings or the probation-officer appointments. It would be another year before she was stopped on a traffic violation and found to be driving without a license—it had been revoked as part of her original sentence—and returned to court.

This time she served thirty days in the county jail, then was cut loose.

By May 2005, Janice was back to the streets and more drugs.

Janice Webb had come close to making it before she fell in love with crack.

She'd graduated from John Hay High School in 1979, and after graduating, she went to work as a waitress at Corky & Lenny's deli, not far from the house where she grew up. It was a respectable place for employment, a local institution that had been around for more than fifty years.

She had a child, a little boy, shortly after graduating high school and did not stick with the father. In 1982, she was busted with stolen property, but prosecutors dropped the charges.

The next year, she met and fell in love with Michael Harrell, whom she married in 1984. The two set about having a life and bringing up her son. Michael was a courier, and they would sometimes travel together around the Midwest. He loved the road. He took her to Los Angeles in 1985 to visit some of his family, making the drive across the country an adventure.

It became even more of an adventure when he found that his own family members had turned Janice on to crack. Michael sent her son back to stay with her relatives in Cleveland, and she developed a habit. By the time the couple returned, both were using.

"See, I cared about her so much that in order for me

to keep her home, I had to buy drugs to be with her," Michael said. "Neither one of us did drugs when we first got married."

In 1986, the couple was busted for theft. Both were declared indigent by the court, and both got a one-year suspended sentence. Janice complied with the terms of her probation, but Michael skipped his probation reporting and ended up back in the slammer.

By then, drugs had estranged the couple, and they divorced.

Janice's life spun out of control. She was arrested numerous times, mostly for drugs and once for carrying a concealed weapon.

She wanted to quit the drugs, but just couldn't. The neighborhood, which by the mid-1990s was an open-air drug market, made it too tempting to resist.

"She tried to get off the drugs and tried to fight it," said her sister, Audrey Webb. "But it was hard for her."

Audrey would know; she herself was busted fourteen times between 1985 and 2007 for hard-core crimes, including robbery.

When Janice was short on cash, which was frequently, since she didn't work, she would hit up her ex-husband, Michael.

"She would always come around when she knew I got a check," he said. He last handed her some cash in February 2009, then never saw her again.

Until June 3, 2009, Audrey would hear from her sister every day, usually by phone, just to check in. Then the calls stopped cold. Audrey filed a missing-persons report a month later. Her missing-person flyers joined the growing number of papers that seemed now to be littering the neighborhood one day and gone the next.

But no one, including law enforcement, seemed to take notice of the proliferation of missing people, all of the same demographic: black women, on the dole, drug abusers, with police records. And all were seen at some point scouring the area around Imperial to feed their habits.

On July 2, 2009, a warrant was issued for Diane Turner, who had failed to show up for a probation hearing in the downtown courts building. In May, she had made a bid to have her supervisory status changed from the onerous "intensive supervision" program to "major drug offender" status. Although neither sounds like much of a deal, when you had fifteen felony drug cases behind you, as Diane did, you took what you could get to free you up to score more easily.

She would still be "on paper," as the street term went, and could be hauled back into court if she tested positive for cocaine, which seemed inevitable. Being on paper meant you still had to check in with the law. Diane had been on paper for almost half her life, dating back to her first bust, in 1991.

In May 2009, Diane had been ordered to attend daily Alcoholics Anonymous meetings for ninety days and three meetings a week after that. If she violated the terms of that order, she would be sent back to prison.

Diane had already been to Laura's Home, the same rehab facility where Telacia Fortson had unsuccessfully tried to reform. She'd been in therapy, community control, the county jail, and several other drug-rehab establishments.

Nothing worked. She was a frequent presence on the streets, an aggressive prostitute.

In a 2000 story in the local *Plain Dealer* newspaper on rehab and life in the county jail, Diane told her support groups, "They said I was never gonna be nothing, and I believed them. I been in and out of here my whole life. I never had no family. I always been by myself."

Hard words from a hard life.

By the age of twenty-four, Diane had had three children, all in the custody of the Cuyahoga County Department of Children and Family Services. Even the loss of her kids wasn't enough to quell her insatiable need for crack. The kids were taken "due to her drug abuse problem and inability to provide proper care and support," according to a county report.

Her fourth child, born in 1994, a daughter, also landed in state custody.

"Mother has had numerous opportunities to involve herself in services," records said. "She has not done this and is not likely to provide for the child in the near future. The child is of a young age and would best benefit from a grant of permanent custody and adoption."

Diane would have two more kids by 2009. She never got custody of them, either.

Diane had little consistency in her life. Plagued by

epilepsy and dubious mental health, she could never go long without drugs.

The one person she held on to was James Martin, a onetime boyfriend who steadfastly took her calls and tried to help her whenever he could.

They would talk on the phone, but the last time they spoke was when she signed off after a call in early September 2009. When he asked around a couple weeks later, no one had seen or heard from her.

James was worried. "Diane always let someone know where she was," he said.

Diane periodically washed dishes at Dailey's, a Jamaican restaurant on 116th Street not far from Anthony Sowell's house. Jasneth Groves, who was foster mother to Denise, one of Diane's daughters, helped her get the job. At one point or another, almost all the women who were rapidly turning up missing would be in there, Groves said.

The Mount Pleasant world was a small one. Many of the people of this world, though sitting firmly on the fringes of society, were at least familiar with each other. They would see each other at the store, at the bus stop, at the social services office.

So when the number of missing women began to mount, people began talking on the street. Although Diane had always been on the fringes, she was always there, getting her hustle on to score some drugs. Things are bad when even the dope hustlers wonder where you are, but that's what went down.

However, no one ever filed a missing-persons report.

*  *  *

There was one more thing, though; when he could get work, James Martin did construction, and in the summer of 2009, he'd found a job working on a house on Imperial, not far from the Sowell home. He noticed a stench, the same smell so many had been complaining about.

"It smelled terrible," James recalled. "It's kind of hard to describe."

That same summer, Anthony Sowell was spending time babysitting the youngest daughter of his former girlfriend, Twyla Austin. Twyla was working mega hours at her sales job at Radio Shack, and he had plenty of time on his hands—stealing tin had night hours, anyway—and so he borrowed some child-care equipment from his sister Tressa's house, which was full of kids anyway.

"He got her a stroller," Twyla says. "He was really good like that with kids, and he really took care of her."

But her daughter would tell her that Sowell smelled bad.

"You know, you can't live in a house with a smell without it getting in your clothes," Twyla says. "I'd imagine if the house smelled, Tony smelled."

So one day, she asked him why she kept hearing that he smelled.

"Ray's Sausage," he said point-blank. And that was as much as he would say about it.


The second week of September, Anthony Sowell got on a bus and headed downtown to Tower City Center, the centerpiece of Cleveland with two luxury hotels, a mall, and restaurants from fast food to foodie playgrounds. He got off the bus and headed right to Charley's Grilled Subs, where his beloved Lori Frazier was working.

She had missed his fiftieth birthday, on August 19, never calling, never stopping by. He was heartbroken.

He stood at the side of the counter, waiting until a few customers moved on, and she came out to meet him. They stood in the mall, among smells of food and the noise of people on a busy weekday, looking at each other.

"As long as we known each other, we never forgot," he said to her. "We never forget our day, birthday, anniversary, nothing like that."

His eyes betrayed his anguish. He turned to leave.

"Stop, let's talk about this," Lori said.

But she said it to his turned back.

# Chapter 11

There's a woman in the alley, and it looks
like she fell out of a window.

**—EMPLOYEE OF FAWCETT BESS**

September 22, 2009, was a cloudy Tuesday, Latundra
Billups remembers.

She was thirty-six years old and in full bloom of a crack
habit that had landed her in jail over the years on charges
of theft, drug possession, aggravated assault, disorderly
conduct, and drug trafficking.

She even procured drugs at times for Anthony Sowell,
the wiry ex-Marine who lived on Imperial. Now that he
was living on his own, his drug needs seemed to have
escalated. Latundra's friend Lori Frazier, Sowell's ex, had
left him, but that didn't mean they couldn't remain
friends.

Latundra was living with her mom on Harvey Avenue,
about eight blocks away, a fifteen-minute walk to Imperial.

"My addiction had taken off," Latundra says. "I was

over to the house on Imperial a lot and that's why; we did drugs. I used to live over there."

She had been over there a week or so earlier with her friend Diane Turner.

"It was the first time she had gone to his house," Latundra says. "I went over there with Nancy Cobb, too. Sowell was so normal; he just liked to get high and drink. He sure wasn't ignorant or stupid. He liked to have girls around—he liked us, I thought."

At 9 A.M. that fall weekday, the Cuyahoga County Sheriff's Office had sent a deputy by the house as part of the random verification of registered sexual offenders and their whereabouts. Sowell answered the door and confirmed, that, yes, he still lived there. And that was it.

Latundra visited first in the early afternoon, left, then came back later. She and Sowell sat on the front porch drinking beer and smoking cigarettes. The talk was the usual, about the neighborhood, about people, and eventually, about Lori.

"He told me I reminded him of Lori a few times," Latundra says.

She was starting to notice that although the house was a spacious three stories, the only place they ever hung out together lately was on the second floor, a mostly empty space that lacked even a working bathroom.

Of course, they had also sat around in his bedroom on the third floor many times, but this departure from the routine, something in the evasive way he looked at her, made Latundra uneasy. Nonetheless, her nature was to be direct.

"Tone, why don't we go up to the third floor?" she asked as the two settled into a couple of straight-back chairs on the second floor later that September evening. She knew that's where he and Lori lived when she was with him. There were bedrooms, a TV, and a working bathroom up there, but down on the second floor, there was just empty space, wooden floors that echoed as they spoke.

"No, it's just too dirty," Sowell said. When she asked to use the bathroom, he provided a white industrial bucket.

*That's very odd*, Latundra thought, but that was all as her mind ripped from the tantalizing effects of the crack.

At one point, Sowell left the house to get some wine before Imperial Beverage closed, at ten. Latundra looked at the door leading to the stairway that led upstairs.

"I was on my way up there," she says. "But as I started to get on the stairs, they were narrow and it was dark, and I turned around. It felt strange."

When Sowell returned, Latundra was still feeling a little uneasy. But she had heard some things around the neighborhood that she wanted to bring up, and although she was all about having a fun time, this seemed as good a time as any to talk about it.

"Some girls around have been talking about you, Tone," Latundra said. "They saying you are a rapist or assaulted them."

Within an instant, Sowell had summoned all of his strength into a single punch to Latundra's temple, knocking her nearly senseless.

"Take off your clothes," he screamed at her as she lay prone on the floor. There was a blanket she had fallen onto, and she groggily obeyed. The whispers that Sowell was a monster were true, she thought in a fog. As she pulled at her pants, she saw him pull a white extension cord out of the wall.

Why would he do that?

Sowell was removing his own clothes, and she noticed his pacemaker, which Lori had told her about. It seemed a strange thing to notice at a time like this. He took the electrical cord and pulled it around her neck. His expression was pure rage.

Then she passed out, and all turned black.

When Latundra awoke, she was still on the floor and Sowell was looking at her as he sat over her in a chair. The extension cord was next to her. Her throat ached, and she knew there was blood. She figured that she had been strangled.

"I'm sorry I tore your sweater," Sowell said. He was partially dressed, and it was still dark out. His voice was a drone, repentant but monotone. "I want to kill you and I want to kill myself. I know I'm going to jail."

Latundra Billups began to talk for her life, but instead of begging, she simply said that she was not going to send him to jail, she wasn't going to tell anyone, and they both needed to get some sleep. She pretended it was just nothing; she was sore, she had been raped, she could feel that, but she was intent on getting away alive.

Sowell lay down next to her and the two drifted off. As daylight wakened them—the curtains on the empty floor were sheer and did little to keep the sun out—Latundra looked at him and he at her.

"I'm sorry. I never meant to hurt you," Sowell said. "I'll have some money tomorrow; I can give you $50 for a new sweater. I can get you high."

He went to the basement and got her a sweater to wear, something to replace her own torn garment.

Latundra played along.

"Sure, that's cool, let's do it," she said. She would call him, she promised as she dressed, calm as could be.

She walked out the front door, calmly unbolting the two locks on the wrought-iron security exterior door, and she pulled a piece of junk mail from one of the two mailboxes fastened just to her left. She wanted to make sure she had the right address. Then she walked across the street to Fawcett Bess's restaurant. And by the time she got in the front door, which was twenty-five feet from Sowell's, she was already crying huge, heaving sobs of trauma and horror. Bess had been a good friend over the years, never judging her, even in her obvious emotional, legal, and physical demise.

"Tony tried to kill me last night," she blurted out. "I played dead; I passed out."

Latundra pulled away the crew neck of the sweater to show him.

"She had these marks on her neck like she had been strangled," Bess says. He told her to call the police right away, and then get to the hospital. "Then I gave one of my workers $5 to get her some beer, cigarettes, whatever she needed."

Latundra accepted the kind offer and headed back to her mother's house, trying to think of what to do. But her mind had already been made up the minute she pulled the mail from the mailbox at the Sowell home. She had his address. She had to report it.

Later that day, September 23, 2009, Bess saw Sowell in the street.

"La La told me that you tried to kill her," Bess said, trying his best not to be accusatorial.

"No, that's not even close to what happened," Sowell said. "What a crazy bitch she is."

After going home, Latundra Billups headed to the emergency room at Meridia Huron Hospital to report that she had been assaulted and raped. She talked to a counselor at the hospital, "And they already knew of him, of Anthony Sowell," Latundra says. "I told them I knew him just as Tone, but they knew that address. They said they had five other women that had come in."

Still, she says, it took weeks before she heard from the sex crimes unit. She spent six hours at the hospital, then was back on the streets, trying to find anything that would blot out the trauma she had endured. Which made it tough for anyone to get in touch with her.

It was the second week of October before she and the police connected, but they dug in, making a case. She gave them times, places, and other details needed to make a good case for an arrest warrant. Detective Richard Durst handled the interview and diligently moved the case through the maddening bureaucracy and inertia of big government law enforcement. He expected he would get his warrant. He just didn't know when.

At the same time that Detective Durst was working the sexual-assault cases against Anthony Sowell, going through the various departments and taking statements, fifty-one-year-old Shawn Morris was working her own deals on the street. With a history of drug abuse, Shawn was a tough woman who knew how to handle trouble.

On Tuesday, October 20, 2009, that's what she found. After a long night of drinking and getting high with a friend, she was sitting at a bus stop on Kinsman when she saw Anthony Sowell. Shawn had seen him around before, and she knew him as a guy who had connections. She had a little cash, and although it was early in the morning, she wanted to keep on getting high. She approached him as he stood at the Key Bank ATM at the corner of 140th Street and Kinsman, about a twenty-minute walk from his house on Imperial.

Sowell agreed to hook her up, and the two had a fine enough time for a few hours that day, drinking beer and wine and smoking crack. By 3 P.M. or so, Shawn headed home to her place on East 143rd Street, an abode she shared with her husband, Douglas. It was a thirty-minute walk but she knew that if she hurried she could catch the Number 14 bus, which would save ten minutes. In her haste, though, she realized that she had left her ID at Sowell's, so she hustled back to grab it.

But as Shawn walked up the stairs—to the third floor, which was now cleaned up—and down the narrow hall to the stairway, Sowell was on her with a choke hold from behind.

"You aren't going home until I say you're going home," he said. He had transformed almost instantaneously into a monster freak, a being possessed with vitriol for Shawn, who had only minutes before bid him a jovial farewell and walked out into the sunshine.

"If you try to scream or run, I'll kill you," he promised, pulling his forearm tight across her windpipe. "Do what I tell you to do or I'll kill you. Whatever I say to you, you better say 'yes sir.'"

It was a warm day, and Shawn was dressed lightly, providing little bulk to protect her from his adrenaline-fueled rage.

He commanded her to take her clothes off and get on the bed, as he removed his.

"Lie on your stomach," he yelled as he moved toward her. He raped her, "Violently," she said later.

When he was done, Shawn started to scream, loudly, bloodcurdling shrieks that tweaked eardrums and beckoned help.

Sowell jumped up and ran first to the room across the hall to the windows, which were open to the Indian summer air. But he failed to notice that one of the two windows in his room was open.

First, she said a quick—very quick—prayer, before leaping from the bed across the room and pushing out the screen, then crawling out, hanging first on the ledge by her fingertips.

"God, I find myself in a predicament," Shawn prayed. "In the mighty name of Jesus, please don't let me die when I go out this window, because I'm about to jump."

Sowell came in and tried to grab her arms and pull her in, but she fell away from the house, down three stories to the narrow alley and the pavement. She crashed with a bone-crushing *thunk*. And then, silence. She had broken both hands and eight ribs, and she had fractured her skull.

But she was alive.

Fawcett Bess again found himself in the middle of the increasing drama at 12205 Imperial. He was working across the street on an apartment over his restaurant when one of his employees came running up the back stairs.

"Bess, Bess—there's a woman in the alley, and it looks like she fell out of a window," the employee said.

Bess ran down the steps and into the street, looking down the narrow patch of concrete between the Sowell house and Ray's Sausage. He saw Shawn, whom he didn't recognize as anyone he knew, lying in a naked heap, and bleeding profusely from her wounds, while Anthony Sowell, also naked, stood over her, trying to pull her to her feet. Which was proving difficult.

Sowell looked sideways at Bess as he struggled with her prone and unconscious body. "It's cool; it's cool," he said distractedly, hoping to get rid of the attention.

"No, it's not cool at all," Bess said angrily. An ambulance

had already been called, and a crowd began to gather at the foot of the alley, on the front lawn of 12205.

Some were taking photos of the scene with their cell phones. Jermaine Henderson, Segerna Sowell's nephew, happened by in his truck as the situation unfolded. He noted the crowd surrounding the prone woman but didn't bother to stop his truck.

"She was on the ground yelling, 'Please help me,' and people were filming her," said Jermaine.

A passerby, Don Laster, finally injected some civilization into the crowd, admonishing them and telling people to put away their phones.

Another passerby, Leroy Bates, came over with a T-shirt for Shawn to cover herself as Sowell continued to try pulling her around the back of the house and up the stairs.

"I can take care of this; you all don't need to call anybody," Sowell told people. "She's my wife. I'm going to take her back into the house."

But police were already arriving, and Sowell stopped. He repeated his story to an officer that Shawn was his wife and said that she fell out the window while they were having sex.

Paramedics took her first into the house, then emerged with her in a full neck brace, with Sowell, now clothed, following them. He hopped into the ambulance for the ride to MetroHealth Medical Center. For all they knew he *was* her husband.

She was out cold by then and couldn't say otherwise.

* * *

At the hospital, Shawn Morris was wheeled into an X-ray room. As she waited, police officers, following up the case, asked her what had happened.

Shawn was a married woman who'd been found naked with another man. She did what many would do in such a compromising situation: she lied.

"I was in the house partying, we were getting high, doing coke, and I dropped my keys off the balcony," she said. It seemed plausible to anyone who wasn't familiar with the house on Imperial, where there was no balcony on the side of the house where she was found.

The scenario was pondered by the cops, and then Anthony Sowell was called into a hallway outside the waiting room. He delivered something close to the same story.

"This is my girlfriend, and yes, we were partying and she fell off the balcony after her keys," he told them. Had they talked at any point before the police questioned them? There was little time for any communication. It was uncanny—unless Shawn had made the whole thing up as a smoke screen to cover for her wayward stray.

The officers contacted their supervisor, who signed off, satisfied. It had just been an accident. Sowell went home later that evening.


A few nights later, Sowell went over to the Cleveland Clinic hospital to see his mother, Claudia, who had suffered a stroke the previous week. She wasn't doing well at all, and the family felt she was in her last days. It pained Sowell to think of losing her. At the same time, his stepmother, Segerna, was also being hospitalized intermittently and was also thought to be close to death. The whole thing was taking him down. Claudia made it, but Sowell left feeling saddened.

He hated to see a death in the family.

# CHAPTER 12

That girl made me do it.
—ANTHONY SOWELL

"At 12205 Imperial, 2nd floor, Cleveland Ohio, Anthony Sowell did force the victim Latundra Billups to engage in sexual conduct. Sowell strangled the victim with an extension cord and raped the victim while the victim was unconscious in his home at 12205 Imperial."

The probable-cause affidavit was signed on October 28, 2009, and when the Cleveland Police Department's Special Weapons and Tactics (SWAT) team met on the second floor of headquarters the next day, Thursday, October 29, at 6 P.M., thirteen members were assigned to the warrant.

There was reason to believe, based on the description of the offense, that Anthony Sowell was a violent offender, and it was possible he would put up a fight.

The plan was for an apprehension, a fairly simple task but one that could go wrong in a hurry. The officers went over a diagram of the house on Imperial, noting that it was a two-family home with a basement and third floor to search as well as the second floor. The first floor was not included in the warrant. The third floor was noted as Anthony Sowell's residence, and the second floor was listed as the place of the alleged crime. Their focus would be on the third floor; they were going there to arrest Sowell.

After the quick briefing, the team members, some clad in black ninja gear and others looking as if they were headed for a day of touch football or a bike ride, gathered in several cars at Luke Easter Park at the western foot of Imperial. It was unseasonably warm; temperatures had hit sixty-five, but the day had born the predictable grayness of fall abutting winter.

One of the team members, Officer Richard Butler, was thirty-four years into his career at the Cleveland Police Department, and had been on plenty of these raids. In fact, he loved them—he'd spent twenty-six years with SWAT. He walked with a swagger, and his graying mustache and receding hairline gave him a muscular dignity. Were he to be portrayed in a movie, Sean Connery might be a good choice to play him.

In keeping with his SWAT team image, Butler led the entry into the house, carrying a shotgun with a lighted scope that cast a bright, wide light. Six officers, including himself, headed straight up the side door entryway to the third floor; five officers went to the second floor, and two went to the basement. All the officers had drawn weapons of various sizes and shapes and were fully prepared to use them if need be; Sowell had already been to prison once, and no one knew if he had a "never take me alive" thing going on.

The officers had no idea whether Sowell would be home, but with this manpower, they would steamroller him regardless.

The officers reached the third floor and split off into each room as they walked down the hall, almost choreographed. As they passed one room, one or two would disappear into the darkness, shouting "Police" at the top of their lungs.

In the kitchen they found a McDonald's bag, with a receipt from earlier that day. The refrigerator was stocked, somewhat, as if someone had shopped for groceries recently.

Two dove into the first room on the right, with its door open. The other two rooms, Sowell's bedroom and the sitting room, had closed doors.

Two other officers opened the door to Sowell's room, where they found a glass crack pipe and some marijuana. There was also mail on the dresser addressed to Sowell. They had the right house, one officer noted to his relief.

Butler walked to the closed sitting room door, stepping on garbage bags full of clothes and debris, and tried the knob. Locked.

The patrolman had been inside a lot of criminal's houses, places with meth labs, months-old garbage, and even bodies. Clearly, 12205 Imperial was a typical crack house and crash pad, with huge chunks of drywall coming loose and the ceiling in the bathroom literally falling down in a big, ripped piece of plaster.

Butler thought he caught a familiar smell—the putrid, gassy odor of death. He had smelled it as he'd entered the floor, and now, as he tried the locked door, the smell was more intense.

It took little to break down the door. Butler's partner gave it a good hard kick while Butler covered him with his shotgun.

They entered the room, and Butler looked to his left and saw two people.

"Police, don't move," he shouted, drawing his weapon on the two.

He adjusted his eyes to the glare his light cast on the individuals. He looked at the windows in the room, which would've looked onto the lights of Imperial, if it weren't for the black plastic taped over them. He looked back at the people on the floor. One had a clover-shaped silver pendant on a necklace on her neck. The other wore a white dress pulled up to the waist, her feet wrapped together in a garbage bag. There was a shovel to the left of the body with the white dress.

He had found Telacia Fortson, last seen in June, and Diane Turner, who was last heard from in September.

Butler paused and flashed his light around the room, doing a quick inventory. He saw a computer table with a PC on it, a dresser, a closet on the right, and a table lamp with a frilly white shade. A brown FUBU work boot lay on its side, maggots crawling in the tread.

At the same time, in the basement, the officers found freshly turned earth beneath the seven stairs, suggesting a grave or at least the start of one. They would soon discover that it was the resting place of Janice Webb.

Butler called for a coroner and headed to get a different kind of warrant, one for murder, not rape. This was going to be even more serious than anticipated.

As emergency vehicles began to arrive, a light rain fell. A police command post was set up, and the media began arriving. By 10 P.M., 12205 Imperial was a full-fledged crime scene, the likes of which the area had never seen.

Cleveland Police Commander Thomas Stacho called a press conference and declared Anthony Sowell a suspect.

"We're asking for the public's help in finding this suspect, Anthony Sowell," Stacho announced. "He is 6 feet tall, 155 pounds, wears eyeglasses, generally wears a mustache, sometimes wears a beard."

Stacho noted that the suspect was a "scrapper . . . he picks up scrap metal and turns it in for cash."

And he ended his announcement by making it known that anyone who called Crime Stoppers and provided information leading to a conviction was eligible for a $2,000 reward.

Debbie Madison didn't wait around to hear that, though. Madison had bought the house across the street from the

Sowells in 2002 and had quickly become fond of Thomas and Segerna Sowell. When Anthony moved in, she befriended him as well.

She knew him as a polite and helpful neighbor, a guy who wasn't even afraid to show her his pacemaker scar while she was trimming her shrubbery one day in 2007.

She had good feelings for him, so when her kids woke her up from a nap around 8 P.M. that evening, telling her that the police found two bodies across the street, she knew she had to find Sowell. That is, if he were still alive.

"We better tell Sowell. He's probably at his sister's house," Madison told a neighbor, who by now was on the street in front of the house with the growing throng, watching the commotion.

Madison quickly drove the few blocks over to Tressa's house, on 130th Avenue, and found Sowell on the couch.

"When I saw him sitting there, he was so nonchalant. At first, I was shocked to see him there," Madison says. "I figured if two people are dead in your house, you should be one of them."

So she said the first thing that popped into her head.

"There are two dead bodies at your house, and the police are there," she told Sowell, who was immersed in a video game with his twenty-two-year-old nephew Ja'ovvoni Garrison.

She began to cry. "I'll take you back over there; you need to talk with the police."

Madison paused uncomfortably. Sowell did not look up. "Maybe there was an accident, someone fell against the cocktail table?" she said hopefully, now fully in tears.

"Calm down; let's go over there," Sowell told her, slowly getting up off the couch. The other kids continued to play and make their usual noise, a symphony of mirth amid the uncovering of evil.

He grabbed his coat, and he and Madison walked to her car. Ja'ovvoni began to get his coat as well. He wanted to go, too, concerned about the worried look on his uncle's face.

But Sowell stopped him. He couldn't leave the kids at home without an adult.

"Wait here; your mom is going to be home soon," Sowell said, then jumped in the passenger seat of Madison's car. On the two-minute ride over there, he said just two things.

"That girl made me do it" was the first thing.

"Now it's all gonna come out" was the second.

Debbie Madison pulled up at the foot of their block, in front of Imperial Beverage, and looked at the blare of lights and law-enforcement vehicles.

"Take me back," Sowell said quietly to her. He said it without any intimidation, and it was not in the form of an order. Just a softly spoken request. But Madison had never felt such tension before.

She did as he asked and dropped him off at Tressa's, then headed back to her house. She parked her car and walked into her house, where her son stood looking out the window at the commotion.

"Tony did it," Madison blurted out.

With that, her son walked out of the house and up to the first officer he could find.

"Anthony Sowell is at a house on 130th Avenue," he said, giving the street number and a quick description of what he was wearing. Madison turned on the TV and all the lights. She began a long, sleepless night.

After Debbie Madison dropped him off, Anthony Sowell walked in the door, grabbed his backpack, and left his sister's house on foot. Within minutes, two Cleveland police detectives knocked on the door.

"They didn't fully explain what was going on; they just said they found a body and asked if we had seen him," Ja'ovvoni says. "Then, twenty minutes later, they came back with another officer and said, 'We know he's here,' like in a movie."

They had Debbie Madison in the car in case they found Sowell and needed a positive ID. The officers did a brief search of the house, but he was gone. They officially had a murder suspect on the lam.

By the next morning, Crime Stoppers and U.S. marshals had put together a $12,000 reward for information leading to Sowell's arrest, upping the cash announced on Thursday night by the Cleveland police by $10,000. The U.S. marshals called in officers from across the Midwest to help Cleveland police look for Sowell.

"We will turn every stone until we find him," U.S. Marshal Pete Elliott vowed, with law-enforcement bravado.

Police and coroners ended their search of 12205 Imperial Thursday night with two confirmed bodies and were still waiting on the results of tests for what would turn out to be the remains of Janice Webb. The crew would be back the next day.

People in the neighborhood were nervous. Random gunshots, murders among drug dealers, and fights over petty arguments were one thing. But a serial killer? That was something else entirely.

"Everybody in this neighborhood is on edge," one local told the *Plain Dealer*. "We want to know what's in the grave. Is this guy a serial killer?"

The scene on Imperial played out hour after hour—newspaper reporters and broadcasters walking the narrow streets of a classic American ghetto, clutching notepads and microphones, desperately trying to interview family members, who were holding vigils and passing out missing-person flyers.

And when Kyana Hunt, Nancy Cobbs's daughter, broke down on camera in the middle of a rather callous television interview—"What if it is her? What if it isn't?"—the camera stayed right on her as she cried and went down on one knee in the street.

After regaining her composure, Kyana said, "All I can say is, if it's not her, tell her I love her and want her to come home."

Police had not yet begun to announce a roll call of the dead.

Friday morning, October 30, 2009, the teams converged again on 12205, and the body count grew. The remains under the turned earth in the basement were determined to belong to Janice Webb. She was found with a green leather belt around her neck, and her wrists were bound with two intertwined white shoelaces, tied so tightly they had to be cut off.

Also in the basement, police discovered a red plastic bucket across the dirt floor from Webb's remains. From the top, it looked like it was filled with newspaper. But wrapped inside the newspaper was the head of LeShanda Long. The bucket had small bite marks around the top rim, evidence of a hungry animal seeking a meal.

Her body would never be found.

The backyard was a killing field. A backhoe was brought in, and blue plastic tarps were erected around the fence line to keep out busybodies with cameras. At one spot, there was a plastic bag sticking out of the dirt, as if someone had just been too tired to complete the burial.

Dogs were turned loose to sniff for cadavers, and the unearthing brought about the eye-watering smell that had been plaguing the neighborhood off and on for years. From that point on, everyone, from officers on security duty to the forensics team, wore masks.

That Friday, the teams found five more bodies in the backyard, women who would later be identified:

Crystal Dozier was found with a slim piece of cloth wrapped around her neck, her wrists and ankles bound with wire.

Tonia Carmichael was also discovered in a shallow backyard grave, an electrical cord around her neck.

Amelda Hunter was back there as well, the strap from a purse cinched about her throat.

Michelle Mason was partially covered in the backyard dirt by blankets and plastic garbage bags. Like Crystal, she had been strangled with a cloth.

Kim Y. Smith, who hadn't even been officially reported missing, was the last of the bodies found in the backyard. She was naked from the waist down, wrapped in black and clear plastic bags, her ankles and wrists tied with strips of cloth.

None of the bodies in the backyard had been buried deeper than twenty-four inches. All were killed by some form of strangulation, be it from a ligature or by hand.

Upstairs, Tishana Culver's body was found in a dirt-filled crawl space in the front sitting room, the same room where SWAT team member Richard Butler had found Telacia Fortson, Nancy Cobbs, and Diane Turner.

Tishana's neck bone was fractured, and her wrists were bound with a knotted rope. She was fully clad in a brown dress, brown pants, shirt, and socks.

And Kyana Hunt's nightmare came true: her mother, Nancy Cobbs, was soon determined to be the fourth body in the front sitting room. She had been strangled, then enclosed in five layers of black plastic bags and wrapped in a comforter. A thirty-six-inch shoelace and a twelve-inch-long white tube sock were wrapped around her neck. Her wrists were bound with another shoelace.

Bottle caps, crack pipes, a condom, cigarette butts, earring posts, and carpet shreds were all found stuffed into bags with and around the victims.

Although the bodies would not be identified immediately, a call went out for those with missing persons to supply DNA in hopes of determining who was being discovered. Inez Fortson brought her six-year-old grandson in to give a DNA sample for Telacia Fortson. There was a growing swell of sorrow among those with missing loved ones, a flush of tragic possibility.

"She had never been gone like this before . . . When I heard about it, I just figured she was there," said Janice Webb's son, Lamarr Webb.

Likewise, Denise Hunter, Amelda's sister, said, "When I seen the house, I knew she was there."

The crime was already becoming one of the biggest serial killings in recent memory. There were eleven bodies found at 12205 Imperial: Tishana Culver, Nancy Cobbs, Telacia Fortson, and Diane Turner in the third-floor sitting room; Crystal Dozier, Tonia Carmichael, Amelda Hunter, Michelle Mason, and Kim Smith in the backyard; and Janice Webb and LeShanda Long in the basement.

Double-digit murders were a tragic benchmark, but most couldn't recall anything like it. Local historians dug in and found the eighty-year-old case of the so-called Torso Murderer, who had savaged an area in Cleveland called Kingsbury Run between 1934 and 1938. The slayer, so named because some victims had been found with their torsos shorn in half, had taken at least a dozen lives. The crimes were never solved.

And now, even as the victim tally grew, police couldn't find their suspect.

The next day, Saturday, was Halloween. The cops were getting nervous as they pulled more bodies from the yard. A Halloween night with a serial killer on the loose? The possibilities made the whole city queasy.

Anthony Sowell spent Thursday and Friday nights in an abandoned house on Martin Luther King Drive, a one-and-one-half-mile walk from his home on Imperial. He had walked over there right from Tressa's. It was a familiar place, one he had scavenged some metal from before. He was carrying a backpack with some warmer clothes, as a cold front had moved through. He slept in a beige spring jacket over a leather zip-up jacket. And he would tell investigators that he drank himself to sleep.

Sowell knew he was a wanted man. But he was also a crack addict, and the booze wouldn't be enough for long. He had to get out eventually to cop again.

On Saturday morning he made his move. He emerged from the house.

For Joe Veal, October 31, 2009, was a great day. Halloween was an occasion to have some fun, and he headed out that morning with a skull mask, his costume for the year. He put it on and decided to take a celebratory drive.

Around noon, Veal was driving down 102nd Street near Mount Auburn, and he did a double take when he saw Anthony Sowell on the street.

"That looks like the guy the police are looking for,"

he thought to himself. Forgetting his mask, Veal stared at Sowell.

Sowell stared back at the man in the skull mask, their glances frozen on each other.

Shaken, Veal headed straight for the Fourth District police station, on Kinsman, about a half-mile away.

In the parking lot, he saw two officers.

"I think I know where the dude ya'll are looking for is at," he said, pulling up his mask. The officers could tell he was serious.

A call to a patrol car just around the corner informed them that the suspect was in the area.

Indeed, the guy the patrolman saw did look a lot like the fellow whose face had been all over TV for the last forty-eight hours. Walking down Mount Auburn, he had a backpack and seemed just like any other citizen. Veal's eye was sharp. For that, he would eventually receive the $12,000 reward from police for assisting in the capture of Sowell.

Cleveland police officer Charles Locke walked up to Sowell and told him to put his hands up and to get on the ground. Sowell gave no resistance, but he looked up from the pavement.

"You got me already. You got me last night," Sowell claimed to Locke, meaning he had been stopped and questioned the previous evening.

Locke disregarded the comment and searched the backpack. In it he found a box cutter, an empty wallet, and a piece of carpet.

"What's your name?" Locke asked him. Sowell told

him his name was Anthony Williams. But Locke wasn't going to let him go until he was sure.

He cuffed him, put him in the patrol car, and called headquarters.

Sergeant Ronald Ross and three other detectives arrived at the scene.

"Is this the suspect?" Ross asked Locke, approaching the car and looking in the backseat.

"We don't have a picture of him," Locke said.

Ross walked back to his car and pulled the APB with Sowell's picture. He looked at Sowell and at the picture, and pulled him out of the backseat.

"You're definitely too close to call on this one," Locke said, referring to the close likeness between the recent photo on the APB and the man standing in front of him.

"I'm not the guy you're looking for," Sowell said again. "The police had me last night and they let me go."

"I have a machine at my office; it's a handheld fingerprint machine," Ross said. "I'm going to check you real quick on it, and if you're not the guy we're looking for, we'll take you wherever you need to go and send you on your way."

It took minutes to fetch the machine, and as Ross began to put the machine on Sowell's finger, he broke down and said, "I'm Anthony."

Detective Luther Roddy, who was watching, asked, "Anthony who?"

"I'm the guy you're looking for; I'm Anthony Sowell."

At that, Sowell broke into a sweat and dropped to his

knees. The bewildered officers looked at each other, first puzzled, then joyous.

*Wow—we just got him*, Ross thought to himself.

The officers helped Sowell to his feet and radioed in. The serial-killer suspect from Imperial was in custody.

Sowell was still sweating and muttered, "I just want to die."

Ross put him in the back of his car for the ride downtown. Sowell seemed to collect himself. The two began having a conversation. He seemed glad it was over, Ross later said.

"Is everything we found in the house all of it?" Ross asked, referring to the bodies.

"I think so," Sowell said.

"What about outside?" Ross said.

"Oh, those," Sowell said.


"Anthony, you a smoker?"

"Yes."

"You want some coffee and a cigarette? I have menthols." Lieutenant Michael Baumiller lit him a Maverick cigarette, since Sowell's left hand was cuffed to the shiny chrome arm of a gray plastic chair. Soon the cuff would be unlocked, but for now it stayed. Sowell sat in the corner of the small interview room on the fourth floor of the Justice Center complex in downtown Cleveland, daylight coming through the half-closed shades.

The room was a converted office, not the formal setting seen on TV cop shows. It had a couple of file cabinets, a computer and a printer on a desk, some chairs on rollers, and a tile floor. On the videotape of his police interview, it looked as if Sowell had stopped by the office of a bureaucrat in some faceless corporate building, not a police interrogation room.

Lieutenant Baumiller, of the sex crimes unit for the Cleveland Police Department, was a rangy everyman with a thick midwestern accent. He was considered a star detective, and the Sowell case played perfectly into his expertise on sexual predators. It was already circulating that there was a sexual element to the crime scene—there almost always was in serial-killer cases—and Baumiller wanted a piece of the action.

He was there because although there were bodies found, the warrant served was for the sexual assault on Billups. That would soon change, but for now, Baumiller and his colleagues were in charge.

Baumiller showed up with a baseball cap and a blue short-sleeved shirt with "POLICE" blared across it in yellow letters.

Two officers brought Sowell, wearing a skull cap and heavy jacket, into the interrogation room, and they waited as he peeled off his outerwear, leaving him in brown jeans, a white half-sleeved jersey, and white high-top running shoes with blue piping.

Along with Baumiller, Sergeant Joseph Rini and Detective Richard Durst sat in the room, talking animatedly with Sowell. They first asked Sowell about Latundra Billups, how he knew her, what might have happened on September 22 that year.

"Well let me ask you, this allegation was made in September and the girl says that you and her went into the house and had some beer and you started messing around and she wanted to stop and then you kind of forced her from there," Durst said. He was avoiding the bigger issue of the bodies, focusing on something relatively lesser.

"That's a lie," Sowell said quickly, softly. "La La. That's who you're talking about."

He explained he knew Latundra—La La—through his old girlfriend.

"Who is your old girlfriend?" Durst asked.

"I'm not going to get her involved," Sowell said with finality. "She ain't got nothing to do with it."

They briefly talked about the rape allegation, and Sowell moved his head animatedly when he talked about it, denying, smoking, fidgeting.

"He was getting agitated," says one of the group of officers watching the questioning on a closed-circuit screen in another room. "He was high and coming down and getting agitated, and now he was thirty-six or forty-eight hours without drugs."

At one point he began to rock back and forth slightly in his chair, both feet on the floor, looking downward as he answered Durst's gentle probing while the other two officers looked on, occasionally tossing in a "Really?" or an "Okay."

The questioning was smooth, asking about his family, about Segerna, his whereabouts for the past couple of days.

"I'm in and out," Sowell said. "I'm mostly, I spend

most of my time over at a friend of mine's house or with my family. Because my mom's in the hospital last week we was all—I remember I spent one night at the hospital, I stayed all night Tuesday. Went Monday night, it was Tuesday morning."

He told them the last woman he was seeing was Shawn Morris, giving them her maiden name of Shawn Smith. No one mentioned the incident of the previous week, when Shawn had "fallen" out of the third-floor window.

Either no one was connecting the dots, or possibly they didn't want to upset Sowell, who was starting to flow with answers to their questions. They knew they had the heavyweight inquisition coming up and wanted him primed.

Then they came back to his recent whereabouts.

"So where you been the last couple of days?" Baumiller asked, easily, testing the waters.

"I was at—I stayed in the house, the house they say they seen me coming out of," Sowell said, referring to the abandoned house. Actually, Veal had seen him walking down the street, but the police had told him otherwise in a bluff.

"Which house is that?" Baumiller said.

"It's like on Martin Luther King Drive. It's a few blocks down from there."

"Is it vacant?" Rini asked.

"Yeah."

"How come you didn't go home?" Baumiller said.

"To my sister's?"

"No, to your house."

"Because I knew you all was looking for me," Sowell said.

"You knew that they were looking for you," Rini said, repeating. "What did you think they were looking for you for? What was going through your head there?"

"I don't know," Sowell said. It was coming to a point here, and he seemed to know it. "They just told me they was looking—somebody said, actually somebody from the area told me."

Baumiller broke the free-flowing banter.

"Hey Tone, this is really, really important. I think you have been pretty honest with us so far, you know what I mean, and probably in the next block of time, 15, 20 minutes, might be the most important 15 minutes of your life. What we're looking for you is to be honest with us some more."

Anthony Sowell didn't move.

"Okay," he said.

"I think you know what I'm talking about," Baumiller said. "Let's just get this over with and talk about what's going on in your home, okay? Now you know we have been to your home."

Sowell stammered. "Okay. What, what?"

"Okay," Baumiller said, his voice getting even-toned and tight. "Upstairs on the third floor where you stay we saw—we found some folks up there. Now, hey, I know it's tough. You know you're running with some people that are kind of fringe folks. It's real important, you're honest with us, you know why you're down here. So what happened up there on that third floor?"

Sowell paused and looked down. He clutched a cup of black coffee in his right hand.

"I just hate what they did to me," he said, low, almost inaudibly. "I'm a nice guy. I feed them and they steal and treat you like shit. Forget about you. I cook hot dogs, French fries, anybody who want to play across the street and play, play down here, play down the street, the rest of the people just come by."

"What pissed you off?" Baumiller asked. "What did these people do to make you angry? Because you know, we are all human beings, we all know that anger. What did these people do to piss Tony Sowell off?"

"My head," Sowell responded. "I don't know what's wrong with me."

The convivial conversation of the first thirty minutes was over. Sowell told of losing control of his temper after he and his girlfriend, whom he still refused to name, broke it off.

"What was your head telling you to do, Tony?" Baumiller asked.

"It's like I was supposed to rape those girls and shit," he said. "People don't give a fuck about nothing, nobody. Even when you help them. I was just—I just—I don't know what happened but I know it had something to do with my last girlfriend."

He went through the story of Lori and her crack habit, of visiting her in jail, of attending her court hearing, and talking with the judge on her behalf.

He stopped just short of admitting that he'd murdered the women. It was what he left implied by the "and shit" at the end of the "supposed to rape those girls" part. That was murder.

"I know everybody going to make me out to be evil, but I'm one of the best," he asserted.

When the police started asking for names, he refused.

"I don't know their names," he claimed, even though he had met some of these women many times.

"I need some time," he said.

The officers offered cigarettes, water, anything to keep him on track.

But he went back to talking about Lori, though not by name, how she'd broken his heart, how he'd cried over the loss of her.

"I love her," he said, staring into space.

Baumiller tried to steer him back to discussing the bodies, but Sowell kept turning the conversation back to his breakup with the still-unnamed Lori.

"That's when I started hearing things," Sowell said. "I mean it was just, I just had like a breakdown or something." He said that the voices told him that "you know what you're supposed to do."

The officers looked at him in a long pause.

"And what, when they said, 'you know what you're supposed to do,' what did that mean?" Rini asked.

Sowell's head twitched back and forth as he sat silently. He dipped his chin, looking downward.

"Try, Tony," Rini urged. "Would you try to tell the voices no?"

Sowell cocked his head to the side, still downcast.

"You couldn't keep 'em back, huh?" Rini said.

Sowell began muttering, almost under his breath, as the officers watched. He was melting down. Then he said, "My mother to this day never told me she loved me. Ever loved me. It's the hardest part."

He raised his head, took a sip of his coffee.

Then he was back, and the officers again urged him to tell them what happened in that house.

"I don't know," he said. "I can't remember. It's like two of me or something. I just don't know. That part is missing."

He shook his head, seeming to pretend he didn't understand anything, almost willing it all to go away. Sowell claimed he'd go into a dream state in which he went under, then would wake up and find everything clean and normal.

"Well, like the people that are dead, there was probably blood on the floor," Durst prodded, trying to get Sowell to drop the act.

"Not when I came to," Sowell replied.

Durst moved on to nailing down the number of victims. By that time, six had been found, with the expectation there would be more.

"Can you guess?" he asked Sowell.

"No."

"If you had to throw a number out, what would you say, like ten?"

"Ten," Sowell repeated leadenly.

"Twenty?" Durst pushed.

"No."

"Not that many?"

"No."

And on it went, settling between ten and fifteen bodies, although Sowell never came out and admitted to having killed anyone.

Eventually, Sergeant Rini, Detective Durst, and Lieutenant Baumiller turned Sowell over to two detectives from the homicide unit, Melvin Smith and Lem Griffin. But there was little change in Sowell's demeanor. He refused to acknowledge that he had killed anyone. The detectives tried the circuitous route, talking about his military service and his pacemaker. They had his handcuff removed, hoping to loosen him up, then moved the topic back to the house. They talked about his leaving the house on Imperial the last time, how he'd left on Tuesday without taking his cigarettes, a full pack.

"I had another pack with me," Sowell explained. "I think my ID and everything. My credit cards."

"Everybody knows that we were there and everybody knows what we were there for," Smith said.

"They are just doing their job," Sowell chimed in.

The detectives were pressing to get these bodies identified as quickly as possible. More and more people were coming forward, asking, demanding to be told the identities of those found. The word swept the streets of the Imperial neighborhood as fast as any crack epidemic.

Although the police were asking for those with loved ones who had been missing and were part of the neighborhood to provide DNA samples, their job would be made much easier if Sowell would start naming names. They knew he knew.

"That's a good thing that you can do is try to identify," Smith said.

"Like I told him, I don't—I don't even remember meeting them, names or anything . . . I just black out."

But finally, Sowell made one break, nothing significant, but mentioned that the last time something went wrong and he blacked out, he'd had an episode.

"I don't know," Sowell prefaced his statement. "A month. Maybe longer than that. September."

Interrogations are like any other interview, provided the subject is willing to engage, as Sowell was. The longer the session goes, the more likely it is to bear fruit.

So Smith and Griffin settled in for some hard work.

"Got you a burger and fries and a drink coming," Griffin told him after stepping out for a while. Smith and Sowell had been talking family and kids.

"You know he's got four grandkids?" Smith said to Griffin.

"Really?" Griffin said, pulling out a pack of cigarettes. "They call you poppa or grandpa?" he asked Sowell.

It flipped the switch for Sowell.

"Uncle," Sowell said quickly, brightly.

"You love that don't you?" Griffin smiled back.

"No, it's ok, but I, everybody calls me that," Sowell said. "And my sister used to get on them for that, said, 'that's not your uncle that's your granddad.' But I said that's ok."

But before the food arrived, the questions began to get more focused and immediate.

Griffin leaned in, smoke from his cigarette drifting upward.

"Yeah, let's make some things right," he said. "It's important. Me, you, and my partner . . . can we go back to our conversation about the bodies in the house?"

"Yes."

"Is there anything specifically that you can remember about the bodies?"

Sowell again went blank.

Next, Griffin read Sowell his rights. Just in case Sowell decided to say something.

Next, Smith tried his hand at cajoling: names, places, dates.

Sowell shook him off.

"This is not going to be pleasant," Griffin said. "It's not pleasant for us and I'm sure it's not pleasant for you. But we know that you concealed some of the bodies, you know that I'm right."

Sowell looked away from Griffin, toward Smith. But said nothing.

Griffin pushed ahead. Again he leaned in.

"Tell me what she might look like. A conversation, her tone of voice, long hair, short hair, black female, white female, Asian—"

"Black female," Sowell said, barely audible.

Smith picked it up there.

"Let me ask you, what about age," he said. "Older female, younger girl . . . ?"

Sowell was tilted in his chair toward Smith, as if he were more receptive to his questions.

"Older," Sowell said, nodding slightly. "20s, 30s."

And with that, the two detectives were rolling.

Without ever confessing to anything, Sowell acknowledged that he met women walking in the neighborhood,
"going to the store, maybe sitting on my porch."

"Can we honestly say, between the three of us, that
the bodies that we found in the house were from people
that you met in that area?" Smith asked.

"I didn't go far," Sowell said, not answering the question directly. "Let's say the Mount Pleasant area, Kinsman
to Buckeye. Not far past 116th."

"And we can honestly say that all of these bodies that
were in your house were females," Smith said, declaring
more than asking.

"Yes," Sowell said.

It went on for hours more. But they had what they
wanted, at least partially: acknowledgment.


Two days later, on Monday, November 2, Detectives
Smith and Griffin pulled Sowell from his jail cell and had
him delivered to the same room. Sowell had a blue zippered jail outfit on, and he sat down in the same chair.
Only this time, although they didn't handcuff him to the
chair, instead of friendly conversation, the exchange was
rancorous.

"You understand what you're here for," Smith said, his
voice no longer the measured timbre of someone asking
a favor. "You know where you are."

He wanted answers. He wanted names. Griffin held
photos of missing women in his hands, and he sat to
Sowell's right in a chair just feet from him, passing the

black-and-white photos to him. Sowell grabbed them, looked at them.

"No," he said. "No. No. No," one after another, and handed them back to Griffin. "I actually don't remember, it's more complicated than you think," Sowell yelled, looking at one photo.

"Explain it to me then," Smith bellowed.

Sowell rose from his chair. "I don't want to explain it," he said, moving toward the door.

Smith, who was sitting in his path, gently put his hands out and pushed Sowell back toward the chair in the corner. Sowell gave them nothing more. But he'd already given them enough.

It was enough, in fact, that John Parker, his court-appointed lawyer, would ask a judge that the interviews be excluded from evidence. He was denied. It was January, two months after the arrest of Sowell.

"We feel his Miranda rights were violated," Parker told a reporter as the state began to assemble its case against Sowell. "He was interviewed by police at great length. I have seen videotape of the interrogations and I have asked that it be excluded."

It was clear that Sowell was Mirandized shortly after the tape began on October 31. But Parker was wisely throwing everything he could in the way of the state's case, much as a man fleeing his pursuers would push obstacles in their path.

Sowell's arrest also set off a flurry of national and international crime checks, tracing the dates he spent time in various locations during his military travels.

Law enforcement in Parris Island, South Carolina; Cherry Point, North Carolina; Camp Pendleton, California; and Okinawa, Japan, looked for cold cases.

In Coronado, California, near Camp Pendleton, after seeing his face on television, a woman claimed Sowell had raped her. Cops in Coronado said they couldn't confirm her allegation because records from that far back had been tossed.

Closer to home, several cold murder cases were revived. The cases were strung together in a timeline with a geographic base that would place Sowell in the area.

In May 1988, Rosalind Garner had been found strangled in her home on Hayden Avenue in East Cleveland. She was a financial analyst who lived alone and had no criminal record. She was found by her sister after she didn't respond to phone calls. In keeping with Sowell's MO, she would have been an unlikely victim.

The other two that were reconsidered, though, had some similarities with the victims who were being discovered on Imperial.

Carmella Prater, a nursing assistant who had once lived on Page Avenue, was discovered dead in an abandoned building on First Avenue in East Cleveland in February 1989. An anonymous caller tipped East Cleveland police to her body. She had been beaten, but the coroner was unable to pinpoint how she was killed.

A month later, the body of Mary Thomas was found by a utility worker in a different abandoned building on First Avenue. She had a red ribbon tightly drawn around her neck. She had been strangled and beaten. Thomas, who was pregnant at the time of her slaying, had been arrested twice for grand theft and spent time in jail.

Both Prater and Thomas had had drug connections, police said. But no ties to Sowell were found.

Anthony Sowell's first court appearance came on Wednesday, November 4, 2009. Accompanied by seven officers and bailiffs, he wore leg and wrist irons and the same blue zippered jumpsuit. He was joined by Public Defender Kathleen DeMetz.

Municipal Judge Ronald Adrine asked Sowell if he wanted to waive his right to an examination hearing.

"That's correct, sir," Sowell said, barely audible, his body leaning forward.

Charged with multiple counts of aggravated murder, rape, kidnapping, and felonious assault, Sowell's bond was set at $5 million.

The next week, on Friday, November 13, Sowell pled not guilty by reason of insanity. It was a plea of convenience and a placeholder until a more solid defense team could be appointed.

Although most cops who came into contact with Sowell after his arrest found him to be curious and sometimes engaging, he turned mercurial when it came to the nuts and bolts of the murder.

By the time he was meeting with lawyers, he had to be aware of what he had told Griffin and Smith, the Cleveland Police Department homicide detectives, during the interrogation immediately following his arrest.

He had *almost* admitted culpability, but a solid defense team would point out that he was a confused addict who was being fed words to acknowledge.

Still, during that session, he said he would wake up some mornings and wonder where the girls went.

"And I'd say, 'oh I let them out last night,' and I'd go back to sleep. If I wasn't drunk or high I'd have no problem remembering and let them out. Or other times I'd wake up and say, 'wow, did I leave them out, did I say good-bye?' and look around to see if they took something."

Insanity is a tough jump from those statements; committing murder while intoxicated is no defense. And although Sowell told both the detectives and then, later, psychologists that he heard voices, such a claim still doesn't meet the criteria for an insanity defense.

It's easy for someone to believe Sowell was insane; that he kept rotting bodies in his apartment while he ate McDonald's would pretty much fit the insanity bill for most of us.

But in the legal world, insanity has been worked over pretty well.

When John Hinckley was found not guilty by reasons of insanity for his 1981 assassination attempt on President Ronald Reagan, the legal definition of insanity was turned on its ear. Laws were passed, and dictates now vary by state. The general assumption is that a criminal might be considered insane if he is "incapable of appreciating his surroundings" because of a commanding mental delusion. And four states—Kansas, Montana, Idaho, and Utah—don't allow the insanity defense, period.

* * *

Anthony's stepmother, Segerna Sowell, died December 19, 2009, at St. Vincent Charity Hospital, a month shy of her seventieth birthday. She never knew what had been found back at her house. She had been living with her mother, Virginia Oliver, but more recently had been moving between hospitals and nursing homes. A small obituary that ran in the *Plain Dealer* noted that she was cremated at H. M. Martin Funeral Home in Cleveland.

# CHAPTER 13

They are treating me well here, I have my own cell and
my own TV so it's ok for now.

**—ANTHONY SOWELL**

Between Anthony Sowell's arrest, the painful confirma-
tion and identification of the bodies at 12205 Imperial,
and the trial, there came a lot of finger-pointing.

Although Cleveland police continued to field ten
missing-persons cases a day, there was a public outcry over
perceptions of police ineptitude and indifference toward
the minority community. Police, though, were not as
much indifferent as they were calloused in handling a
culture of crime that defied all solutions.

Meetings, demonstrations, and public floggings
wouldn't fix that. Crime kept on happening around the
city.

But crime on Imperial came to a screeching halt. No
doubt it had something to do with the police cars that
were now a part of the landscape.

*   *   *

Embittered families discovered that police had let Anthony Sowell go on several occasions only to find that he had killed after being set free.

The first lawsuit came in May 2010 from Florence Bray, Crystal Dozier's mother, against Anthony and Segerna Sowell. It was wisely filed preemptively to ensure that Sowell could not benefit from any media exploitation of his story. It was a pure motive for Florence, who asked for minimal damages from a defendant who had nothing.

Shawn Morris and her husband, Douglas, filed a lawsuit in November 2010 against WOIO Channel 19 in Cleveland. It claimed that the TV station publicized her attack at 12205 Imperial, noting her criminal record, "including charges of solicitation and drug possession." It also alleged that the station portrayed her as an associate of Sowell's, someone who "had knowledge of his other criminal activities, including the murders of multiple victims."

It also erroneously claimed that Morris was not a public figure and alleged invasion of privacy. The action sought damages of more than $25,000, but the case was eventually dismissed with prejudice, with WOIO being awarded attorney's fees.

In December 2010, Gladys Wade sued everyone, from Cuyahoga County to Loretta Coyne, a Cleveland city prosecutor who'd cited a lack of evidence in Gladys's case and had declined to bring charges. Gladys also sued several detectives and the city of Cleveland.

She also attacked the practice of straight release, under which offenders are let go because of a lack of prosecutorial evidence in hopes of securing such evidence later but in practice let potentially dangerous characters go free. Which is what she claimed in her suit had happened with Sowell after he assaulted her.

Gladys Wade asked for yet-undetermined damages.

Also in December 2010, relatives of Janice Webb, Nancy Cobbs, Amelda Hunter, Diane Turner, and Telacia Fortson filed a suit against the same Cleveland police detectives, Coyne, and the City of Cleveland. Their allegations were about the same as Gladys Wade's.

Donnita Carmichael, Tonia Carmichael's daughter, also filed a suit, in January 2011, naming everyone possible as a defendant, but chiefly the City of Cleveland. The suit accused general ineptitude regarding the policing of Anthony Sowell's conduct and the continued failure of police to home in on Sowell as the culprit in the string of missing persons. The suit specifically noted the smell that it claimed permeated the neighborhood, the Gladys Wade episode, and the city prosecutor's failure to file charges against Sowell in relation to that kidnapping and assault.

"The actions of defendants in releasing Anthony Sowell on December 10, 2008, were reckless, wanton and willful and, as approximate cause, the plaintiff's deceased relative suffered terrible torture and death that could have been avoided and upon knowledge it is believed that Anthony Sowell kept Tonia [Carmichael] alive and first raped, tortured her, as well as all of his victims before murdering them, and Tonia [Carmichael] was alive at the time of Sowell's arrest and was not murdered until on or about December 10, 2008."

Donnita sought $42 million in damages.

Also in January 2011, U.S. Representative Marcia Fudge, whose district included the Imperial neighborhood, announced support for a memorial for the victims and pledged she would look into whether local officials had complied with the Violence Against Women Act of 1994.

The act allocated public money to ensure the perpetrators of violent crimes against women were properly prosecuted and also provided money to victims of crime against women. Passed in 1994, it was reauthorized in 2000 and again in 2005.

In February 2011, she met the families of some of the Sowell victims during a town-hall gathering in her district, and in May 2011, Fudge issued a resolution of condolence for the victims as part of a rally outside the Cleveland Heights City Hall. And on Labor Day weekend, Fudge attended the Ohio Eleventh Congressional District Labor Day parade, where eleven doves and one thousand balloons were released in honor of the eleven murder victims.

"We are releasing their spirits to a higher place, but we are also releasing our hurt and our anger to a higher place," Fudge proclaimed.

But Fudge, outspoken as she was for the families, neglected to mention one thing: she was distantly related to Anthony Sowell. In fact, she most likely had been to 12205 Imperial at some point in her life, since Anthony's aunt Mildred was Marcia Fudge's sister-in-law. Up until 1995, ten years before Anthony Sowell would arrive, Mildred Fudge had even been on the deed to the house.

"Timothy Fudge, my uncle, married Mildred, who was my father's younger sister," says the younger Thomas Sowell. "And Timothy was the brother of the congresswoman."

It was one of those things that slipped through the media transom.

Anthony Sowell spent some time writing letters to a website devoted to selling serial-killer memorabilia called Serial Killers Ink. One of his letters went up for sale for $200. He addressed the letter to employees at the California-based outfit. In one letter he wrote, "I can only get money orders at this time and yes, I can receive pictures."

On a Christmas card, he wrote to one admirer, "So if you need someone to talk to I am here for you. So tell me what do you want to know about me? I know what I want to know about you, what type of woman are you? Do you have a man in your life?"

Beneath his signature was the Bible verse Matthew 1:23: "Behold the Virgin shall be with child and bear a son and they shall call him Emmanuel, which means 'God is with us.'"

Still another, to a California woman, read, "Thank you

for sending me your support. I hope that you are doing well and in good health. I am in need of just about everything and anything you can do to help out is a blessing . . . never send cash in the mail, you can send me money orders. Just put my name and number on it and put it in with your next letter. OK, I've got to close now, I only get 20 min out."

He signed it "Tony Sowell" and underneath, "Anthony Sowell."

To a person named Barry, he wrote about his life in jail.

"They are treating me well here, I have my own cell and my own TV so it's ok for now . . . I was married before, my ex-wife died in an industrial accident back in 1998 in California, her home state. We were married for about three years and had no kids."

He signed off, "Your pal, Anthony Sowell."

The letters sold for between $80 and $200.

# CHAPTER 14

You have to call me master.

**—ANTHONY SOWELL**

As investigators pieced together Sowell's trail of terror, they uncovered a tale that was as frightening as it was infuriating.

The prosecution was pulling together any other incidents that Sowell might have been involved in and was casting a wide net to include reports of unsolved cases from police departments in the area.

It was already discovered that Sowell's name was known to some of the sex crimes investigators before his arrest, although no one had pinned any unsolved sexual assaults on him. The eleven bodies were likely enough. But as with any good prosecution team, enough was never enough.

When Sowell was arrested and his face plastered across every TV in the city, in October 2009, Keshana Murray†

---

† Denotes pseudonym

called the Cleveland Heights police and left a message. It was him—that's her attacker from that previous April, she said. When police tried to get back to her, she was unreachable.

Word of the call trickled up to the prosecutor's investigation team. They found that the attack would have been three days before Amelda Hunter disappeared, and five days before the attack on Tanja Doss. It portrayed a man in a violent frenzy.

And it was textbook Sowell.

On the afternoon of Friday, April 17, 2009, Murray walked into Hillcrest Hospital on Mayfield Road and told the receptionist at the desk that she had been raped and needed help. Murray couldn't have come to a more proficient place in Hillcrest, at least on paper.

The hospital, like most others in the area, was part of the Cleveland Clinic. In 2003, Diane Daiber put together the Sexual Assault Nurse Examiner program for the clinic at Hillcrest. Daiber was a devoted advocate, nurse, and caregiver for sexual-assault victims, and she had spent the last twenty-four years at Hillcrest. Comfort and justice were her games, and she played them well. Murray was in good hands.

She told a story that, on its own, was simply a victim's tale of falling into the hands of one more depraved predator on the bad streets of Cleveland. There was nothing to make Daiber, or later on, the police, believe that Murray's assault was committed by a serial predator.

It was simply disturbing on its own merits.

Murray said that less than forty-eight hours earlier, on

April 15, around 9 P.M., she was waiting for the Number
40 bus at a stop in the Superior Avenue and Glenmont
Road area of Cleveland Heights, about four miles north
of Imperial Avenue. Her place, on Kensington Road, was
about two miles away, but the bus would drop her within
sight distance.

As the thirty-nine-year-old woman waited alone, a blue
Dodge Neon pulled up to the stop, and the passenger-
side window rolled down. It was a girl she knew only as
Monique, an old friend she knew from the streets and as
a co-tenant at the Forest Hill Park Apartments from a few
years back.

"Where you going?" Monique asked, her breath coming out in white condensation puffs. It was around forty
humid degrees, and a ride home would be better than
taking a bus anytime.

Murray jumped in the backseat of the car, and Monique
introduced her to the driver. He was unremarkable looking to her; she never did remember his name. A black
gentleman, wearing a green dress shirt, khakis, brown
leather coat. His hairline was receding slightly, and he
had a shadowy beard. And one other thing: his eyes,
Murray would later describe, were yellow.

She would later learn she was describing Anthony Sowell.

While Monique and Murray chatted, he drove them
to a Walgreens on Mayfield Road, a two-minute ride.
Monique jumped out and was gone; she had errands to
run and would get a bus home.

Murray got into the front seat and told Sowell her
address—Kensington Road—about two miles away. But

as the car headed south on Superior, Sowell made a quick right turn onto a side street, taking them away from the most direct route.

"This is the wrong way, the wrong turn," Murray said, trying to help. Perhaps he was confused.

With that, Sowell turned half toward her and, with an open hand, slapped her across the temple, knocking her glasses onto the seat.

She was in trouble. She didn't know this guy, and now she was being kidnapped.

She held on as he made a series of erratic turns, twisting the five miles south as if evading an invisible pursuer. Her body jostled in the seat as he turned, and she tried to figure out where she was. Murray was half dazed from being struck, and she was also almost breathless that this was happening to her. After fifteen minutes, the car pulled into a narrow driveway in a place she didn't recognize. The house was a three-story duplex, and in the dark, it looked to be a brown-brick dwelling.

Murray had regained her composure and was trying to notice these things. She feared for her life, but if she made it, she sure as hell wanted to make sure this guy was caught.

But before she could think about jumping out of the car and running, Sowell had run out of the car and around to her side, pulling her hair and grabbing her in a choke hold while dragging her to a side entrance to the duplex. Her fight was futile; he was amazingly strong for a smaller guy—she could see that he wasn't a big man now that he was out of the car.

Murray scanned the area as they got to the top of the stairs. He pushed her through a small kitchen area with a table and two chairs and down a narrow hall to a bedroom on the left. On a large dresser, she noticed some items that didn't bode well; a crack pipe, a filet knife, some sexual lubricant, and some lottery tickets.

But there was something else that permeated the place: an overwhelming smell of rot, something fetid and gaseous and horrible, like mold or old garbage.

She later described it poignantly as "stagnant."

"You have to be trained like an animal," Sowell told her. "And you have to call me master."

He ordered her to remove her clothing. Terrified, she obeyed. And for forty-five minutes, Sowell sexually assaulted her in all ways possible.

And when he stopped, he continued to yell at her and, indeed, treat her like an animal.

"I am a trained killer; I was in the Marines," he told her. Sowell would begin a sentence, then stop, and begin a whole other thought. He was in a full manic episode, and over the next thirty-six hours, she was subjected to sexual assaults four times. She was a captive, tied to a chair in the bedroom with dress ties when he wasn't abusing her.

"Do you like to do Ecstasy?" he asked her after the first rape, referring to the mild hallucinogen. He had just returned from the store and carried a bag as he walked into the bedroom. In it were some bottles of King Cobra malt liquor, some rotgut wine, and a pack of cigarettes.

She realized that the attacks were not even close to

over as Sowell poured together a sickening blend of the beer and wine. She knew what was next; he made her drink it and forced a pill into her mouth. With her hands bound, she could not fight what she kept thinking was some kind of super-adrenalized strength that her attacker was gathering from his role as "master."

As daylight broke on Friday, April 17, Murray awoke and saw the light streaming around the blanket that covered most of the two side-by-side windows in the bedroom. Sowell dozed peacefully, his left arm draped over her, as if the two were just another limb-tangled couple.

She couldn't bolt; the hallway was too long, and she was sure he could catch her. But he was out pretty good, given the drinking and drugging he had done the night before.

Murray eased herself out from under his arm; she slid her jeans and sweater on, watching her captor the whole time. He moved slightly. She could knock him out, she thought, given the drop she had on him now.

Murray grabbed a framed picture from the wall; she was impressed with his attention to home decor, in fact. It was an ivory frame with glass, and—*whack!*—she clubbed him over the head with it as he groggily looked up.

He was dazed only slightly and jumped up and on her as she tried to run out the bedroom door. Murray picked up a piece of glass from the broken frame and jabbed him on the neck with it as he moved toward her. They began to fight as she ran down the hall for the stairway door, with Sowell putting his arm around her neck from behind, just as he did when he brought her up to this den of horror on Wednesday night. This time, though, Murray had it figured out; she bit his forearm, hard.

He was bleeding profusely as she ran down the stairs, that she knew. She had looked at him and saw her handiwork; the glass shard had cut him deeply.

Murray ran down the back stairs and came out the side door of 12205 Imperial—that's exactly where she was—and began a panicked run.

She was unable to later recount her four-and-a-half-mile run home in a terrorized haze. But she made it by 9 A.M. or so and called a friend. By 9:30, Murray was at South Pointe Hospital, from which she was transported to the emergency room at Hillcrest. It was there she met with Diane Daiber, who called police. Because Murray was picked up in Cleveland Heights, which borders the city of Cleveland, the Heights police were called.

As patrol units sought Monique and some of the locations Murray had detailed in her account of the abduction and assault, Murray was treated for her injuries. A sexual-assault kit was placed into evidence.

The kit is key in catching rapists, and its contents are usually collected by a specially trained nurse. These kits usually contain biological evidence that can be tested for DNA to apprehend a suspect.

In this case, it was Murray's jeans and bra that were put into the kit as evidence. Nurses also took blood and urine samples from Murray, which was standard procedure.

They handed the rape kit to police investigators. All were then given to the Lake County Crime Laboratory for testing, then to enter the DNA in a criminal database to see if there were any positive hits.

And police obtained the security surveillance tape from Walgreens for the time Monique was dropped off by Sowell.

Police investigators, though, hit a dead end. They tried rental-car records for a blue Dodge Neon and called the complex, Forest Hill Park Apartments, at which Murray and Monique lived at one time. They traveled with Murray to the areas she thought she was in when she was abducted, during that crazed ride back to the three-story house.

Nothing.

And there was never any DNA put into any database.

That's because there were actually two sexual-assault kits given to police in one bag. The one with the blood and urine from Murray were given to the lab. The other, which potentially bore the DNA of her attacker, was not part of the drop at the lab.

When the lab opened the box that it thought would contain the evidence, the jeans and the bra, it found only the blood and urine of the victim "rather than being a sexual-assault kit as described on the evidence submission form," according to a report dated May 5, 2009.

The lab called police "so we can discuss how to proceed." The detective called back and told the lab to test the blood and urine.

As for the jeans and bra, someone just assumed it was evidence, which belonged in the evidence room.

Murray fell out of pocket shortly after her assault, and police claim they tried to follow up with no success in

September 2009, when Cleveland police inquired about the case; they had a similar rape and had heard about this unsolved assault.

In March 2011, the Cuyahoga County prosecution team contacted Cleveland Heights about the case. What ever happened with that other evidence?

A Cleveland Heights detective hit up the evidence room and found the bag with what police had in 2009 called "a second rape kit." Actually, it was the evidence needed to get the DNA of the perpetrator. It had never been tested.

There was no mea culpa from Cleveland Heights.

The city's law director, John Gibbon, claimed that the evidence was handed over in two batches, "utterly unexpected."

The first batch was the blood and urine of the victim; the second, the kit with the DNA evidence.

"We've never seen that," Gibbon said. "We don't know why that was done."

And, as if to wash its hands of a grievous error, the city issued a statement:

"Had the second rape kit box which was in a package of clothes been discovered and analyzed in 2009, there would have been no match with Mr. Sowell's DNA in the State's DNA Bank since Mr. Sowell's DNA was not in the State Bank at that time."

Which was true; through one more epic episode of bureaucratic ineptitude, Sowell's DNA, collected during his first prison stint, was never entered into the national DNA criminal database.

The sample was collected by the state prison system and sent to Fairfax Identity Laboratories, in Fairfax, Virginia. The lab was hired by the state to conduct DNA coding and freeze blood samples under a contract while Ohio was building its own lab, in 1990.

Fairfax Identity Laboratories is owned by AIBioTech, a large firm that today holds a number of federal government contracts.

The state claimed the sample was sent to the lab but it was never returned to the state. "I don't know if it got lost in the mail or if it got lost in the Virginia lab," said Eve Mueller, a spokeswoman for Attorney General Mike DeWine. "Nobody knows what happened to it after that."

It seemed that no one was all that interested in competence when it came to the women who fell prey to Anthony Sowell. They were truly, as far as the Establishment was concerned, nobody's women.

Then there was the curious case of Vernice Crutcher, a longtime felon who claimed that she was raped and beaten by Sowell in a 2006 crime.

Crutcher was the subject of a book, called *I Survived the Cleveland Strangler*, written and self-published by a man calling himself CD Newton, or Charles D. Newton.

The book chronicles the story of Crutcher in a sketchy, streetwise chatter. Newton portrays himself as an ex-boyfriend and now advocate and "caregiver" for Crutcher, hoping to get her off what has been a multi-decade addiction to drugs.

There is little doubt to the allegation, which was published in the *Plain Dealer* in June 2006, that she was raped in an empty house in the Imperial area by a man in his thirties.

Crutcher provided a sketch of her assailant, which ran in the June 30 *Plain Dealer*, and, in hindsight, looks much like Sowell.

And the situation was very similar as well. Crutcher claimed to have met the man she was now saying was Sowell near Kinsman, where he promised to get her high on crack and pay her for sex. He took her to the abandoned house and raped and beat her.

Newton's book assailed Cleveland police for failing to follow up on Crutcher's case.

"The Cleveland Sex Crimes unit has covered up Vernice Crutcher's cold case by engaging in obstruction of justice," the second page of the book blares. "Why? They don't want you to know that they had nearly a year to capture Sowell before he started his killing spree."

His allegations also extended to the murder of Magdalia "Lucky" Roulette, who was murdered in August 2005, her body found near 79th Street. Roulette lived in Kinsman, about a mile from where Sowell was living in Slavic Village with his sister and a slew of kids at the time.

Newton made grandiose claims in the book, which was marketed with savvy acumen via online ads during the trial.

"I deeply owe it to the eleven women of Imperial Avenue to reveal the truth," Newton wrote. "I knew years before their deaths that Vernice's attacker from June 18,

2006, if not captured, would strike again. . . . Due to her surprised survival the Cleveland Strangler Anthony Sowell changed his strategy and started luring women to his home."

Newton registered his company, Double or Nothing Productions, in 2007 for "artistic productions in theater and film," he said in state records. He had published an e-book in fall 2010 called *Foreclose the Predators*, a courtroom drama.

*I Survived the Cleveland Strangler*, also an e-book, was given out promotionally, protected by a password, then put up for sale at Amazon as a download for $2.

Vernice Crutcher's adult crime record dates back to 1975, when, at eighteen years old, she was arrested for grand theft.

In 1978, she was arrested for felonious assault and sentenced to one to five years in state prison. Crutcher was out by early 1981 and reoffended with another grand-theft case. She was sent back to prison.

And this is the course of her life as recently as 2011, when the book came out as a download.

Court records for Cuyahoga County show Crutcher with the address of an apartment building (in Euclid, and dating back to 1975) that Newton now presents as his home, although in his book, he contends he met her around 2004.

The book made a minor stir in the community, but Cleveland police said the book's claims had no merit after a DNA test cleared Sowell of the 2006 case.

*   *   *

Sowell's DNA was not entered into the national database when it was supposed to be, but it wouldn't have mattered. How many other criminals have escaped detection, or had delayed detainments, because of such a massive screwup?

The Sowell case exposed all the holes in the system. And the women on the streets of Cleveland and their families were paying for it.

There was another line of chatter going on in the black community as the trial approached. Black leaders, as well as citizens, were justifiably upset at the bungling of law enforcement, which had failed to arrest Sowell on several occasions, most notably the Gladys Wade assault. Community members were also angry over the perception that cops didn't care about black people, a mistaken notion but one that has had traction for generations.

And among a subgroup of these complainants, the name Arthur Feckner came up. Feckner was a white drug dealer also known as White Art among the black community. With a good source in Miami, Feckner moved a lot of cocaine in Cleveland, much of it among the black community.

Feckner also had a number of charges dating back to 1975, including drug trafficking, larceny, possession of drugs, and receiving stolen property.

So after being busted once again in 1985, Feckner agreed to turn snitch in order for leniency, working for a specialized narcotics unit in the Cleveland Police Department known as the A-Team.

But before he could begin his work with the A-Team, Feckner told police he had a $560,000 debt he had to pay up with his Miami connection. And to do that, he had to sell more drugs.

Thus, while working with the Cleveland police as a drug informant, Feckner also sold drugs out of an eastside house across from the housing projects, about three miles from Imperial Avenue.

Police later said they thought Feckner was making the money by collecting on old debts.

The A-Team, working with cash from the DEA, was targeting the Miami connection, a big-time score that would reflect well on the department and help some political ladder climbers in the department move forward.

The bust was deemed a success at the time: fifteen people arrested, six of them convicted, and forty-six kilos of coke taken off the streets.

Cleveland Mayor George V. Voinovich, along with a couple of the agents making the bust, posed with the money and drugs for a photo.

But shortly after the celebration had died down and the details of the operation began to come out, some people began to realize that Feckner was selling drugs to the black community for the political gain of law enforcement.

U.S. Congressman Louis Stokes in 1990 told hundreds of people in the black community at a Cleveland church about his investigation into charges that Cleveland police allowed Feckner to sell cocaine to blacks on the east side. He said that police used money from the drug sales to finance an operation that eventually captured Feckner's suppliers.

"What happened with Feckner . . . are troubling reminders of things permitted to happen in America's black community that wouldn't be tolerated in the majority community," Stokes told a reporter at the time. "You can search history, and you simply don't see this happening in white communities."

Five Cleveland police officers were indicted on drug-trafficking charges.

At the trial, a Cuyahoga County prosecutor said the cops were more concerned with making a possible bust down the line than with keeping drugs off the street.

Two ex–drug cops testified that one of the five on trial, Sergeant James Bistricky, who headed the A-Team, had told them to keep their men away from the area where the drug sales were going on, indicating that he knew they were taking place.

The judge in the case granted the defendant's motion for acquittal, and they walked.

The black community felt like it was being marginalized. But nothing ever happened as a result.

And here in 2009, it once again felt like no one cared about crime in its midst. Sowell preyed on the black community just as Feckner had, with a nod and a wink from the Cleveland cops.

# Chapter 15

There are fourteen main victims. . . . Eleven that are
dead and three who lived to talk about it.

**—CUYAHOGA COUNTY ASSISTANT
PROSECUTOR RICHARD BOMBIK**

For all the fanfare and attention, murder trials most often
go down with few surprises. Most people, both those
involved in the trial and the spectators, have their own
ideas of what happened and who did it and why.

Anthony Sowell's trial was clearly along that line. He
was a dead man walking well before the trial began with
jury selection in June 2011, after two previous delays.

Although there was media interest, his trial also coin-
cided with that of Casey Anthony, the pretty young
woman in Florida whose two-year-old daughter, Caylee,
turned up missing, then dead, in 2008.

Her case had a whodunit element that was indeed compelling, while the case in Cleveland was pretty standard,
or as standard as the wholesale slaughter of eleven women
could be.

Casey Anthony was white, twenty-two, and loved to party in nightclubs.

Anthony Sowell was fifty-two, black, and smoked crack and drank King Cobra.

The result: while Casey Anthony's case was carried live by CNN at some points, there was little coverage of the Sowell trial outside of Cleveland.

But as open and shut as the Sowell case might have seemed at the outset, there would be surprises along the way, starting with a petition to accept a guilty plea signed by the families of eight of the eleven victims, and ending with Sowell's taking the stand on his own behalf.

The state brought on two prosecutors with vastly different records and backgrounds to deliver a guilty verdict for the people.

Richard Bombik was a white older man, set to retire until this case came along. He was a steady toiler in the courtroom and out, his blue eyes and white hair driving home his dignified elder-statesman air.

But in a town with mostly poor-on-poor violent crimes, Bombik prosecuted mainly ghetto slayings and passion shootings, heartbreakers like the mother who killed her four-year-old daughter.

But if Bombik was the sage, the star of the state was Pinkey Carr, a forty-five-year-old black female who was also running for a county judgeship, though in doing so, she'd had to forsake her book club, golf, and her travels, three of her favorite hobbies.

Instead, she would get up at 4 A.M., hit the gym, and be downtown in her ninth-floor office at the Justice Center by 6:30.

Carr had devoted herself to the cause of putting guilty people in prison. She got the legal bug when she was a toddler; when she was three years old, Perry Mason on TV drew her attention like no other character.

She graduated from Cleveland's John F. Kennedy High School, where she was a "high stepper"—"Like a majorette, but I didn't carry a baton," she explains—and went on to Baldwin-Wallace College to earn her bachelor's degree in political science, followed by law school at Cleveland-Marshall College of Law. Shortly after law school, Carr scored a job as an assistant prosecutor with the City of Cleveland. Promotions came quickly, and she became chief counsel for the city's law department just as the city became mired in political scandal over questionable promotions by outgoing mayor Michael R. White, in 2001. She left the city around the same time White did only to get a call from Cuyahoga County Prosecutor Bill Mason in early 2002. He posed a simple question: would she come back? She returned, and within two years, Carr was part of the team handling major trials.

Her colleagues became both friends and educators. She looked at Bombik as a mentor, "and a great lawyer," she says.

She and Bombik had worked together before; in 2004, they handled the rape-murder trial of Daniel Hines, whose victim was an eleven-year-old girl, though that eight-week trial had ended in an acquittal.

Carr, in the meantime, had socked away some victories. She got a life sentence for a cop killer in 2008, and in February 2011, as a deputized U.S. attorney, she helped convict an arsonist who'd set a blaze that killed nine people.

Anthony Sowell's defense team came down to two relatively unknown attorneys named John Parker and Rufus Sims.

Parker was a quiet veteran of the defense-attorney ranks. Born in 1962, Parker grew up in Belpre, Ohio, on the West Virginia border in the southeast corner of the state. His first move away from home was to Columbus, where he earned his undergrad degree at Ohio State University. His second move was to Cleveland, where he attended law school at Case Western Reserve. He liked the city well enough; in 1991, he bought a house, took a job as a public defender with Cuyahoga County, and struck out on his own as a defense attorney.

He had plenty of death-penalty trial experience, with some considerable success. In 2007, Parker represented Vernon "Broadway" Brown before the Supreme Court of Ohio. Brown, who carried a .45 caliber handgun he called Mike Tyson, had received death for a 2004 street murder. Parker convinced the court that the prosecution had withheld witness statements that could have helped the defense. In a retrial, Brown was convicted on murder charges and received a life sentence.

In the defense world, that's a victory.

But Parker had also unsuccessfully represented Kenneth Biros in federal appeals. Biros in 2009 became the first person in American history put to death by a single drug rather than the usual three-drug cocktail. The new one-drug method was used to stem a lawsuit that claimed the three-drug system was painful for the prisoner.

Parker, a strident foe of the death penalty, attended the execution.

And when the call came for the Sowell case, Parker realized he had another shot at saving someone from death. He accepted quickly.

The Sowell case was a career maker as well, and at age sixty, Rufus Sims was smart enough to realize it.

When Cuyahoga County Judge Eileen T. Gallagher summoned Sims to the arraignment room at the courthouse shortly after Sowell's arrest, Sims had feared he was going to be chastised for something or other, though he and Gallagher had a cordial relationship.

Sims had three years earlier defended the judge on national TV when the judge threw a rape case out after the prosecution was late to court. Gallagher and Sims had gone on CNN as a guest of Nancy Grace in the wake of the judge's action, where Grace indelicately berated Gallagher. Sims, who was representing the defendant, supported Gallagher's decision.

Now, the usually abrupt judge told Sims to sit down.

"I'd like you to represent Anthony Sowell," Gallagher said.

The words couldn't get out of her mouth quickly enough. Nor could Sims get his yes answer out any faster.

"I didn't hesitate," Sims says. "I really wanted it. It was a make-or-break a career case."

Born in 1951 in Cleveland, Sims was a black man who'd grown up in the civil rights era, when his father had to ask a white man to buy milk at a store that refused to sell for blacks.

"I realized that law was an effective way to create change," Sims says.

He'd been raised on the city's east side, a couple miles from the Imperial area. He went to Glenville High School and then joined the U.S. Air Force in 1971. Sims took undergraduate classes throughout his military assignments in a number of locations, including San Antonio, Miami, and San Diego, then attended law school at Cleveland State University.

He passed the bar in 1988 and had worked as an assistant prosecutor in East Cleveland before opening his own defense law practice. Sims was an ACLU member and a strident foe of the death penalty.

Both he and John Parker knew that they had the case of their lives.

They filed motion after motion in a blur of paperwork, asking for mental evaluations, paging through Anthony Sowell's military and high school records, going over surveillance video taken of the neighborhood by five cameras put up by Ray Cash, owner of Ray's Sausage, next door to 12205 Imperial.

A year into the trial preparation, the team had already run up the highest bill ever for a defense team in Cuyahoga County.

The judge, Dick Ambrose, of the Cuyahoga County Court of Common Pleas, was in a tight spot, though,

both financially and politically. To refuse the fiscal over-
tures of the defense team was to risk an appeal on the
grounds of a lack of funds to mount a proper defense.

At one point, Parker and Sims asked for $62,000
toward the cost of mitigation experts, people like psychologists who could testify to the defendant's state of
mind and the effects of his upbringing and environment.

Ambrose refused them, writing in his opinion, "Clearly
the defense team has put considerable effort into justify-
ing its proposed budget to the court. But to attempt to
interview 198 individuals in order to prepare a mitigation
case, at this point, seems excessive to say the least."

Although they struck out on a number of requests, by
December 2010, they had rung up $185,000 in costs.

They tried all the standard maneuvers to keep moving
the trial back, creating as much time as possible between
the crime and the trial, a traditionally sound defense move
to remove emotion and familiarity, especially in this case,
given the gravity and emotional nature of the crimes. Sims
and Parker filed the standard motions for delays, moving
the trial out of the county, and continually asking for more
money.

After two extensions for the trial were granted, in February and May, jury selection finally began on Monday,
June 6, 2011.

But the families of the victims had been talking among
themselves. Some of them were done crying, and it had
been eighteen months since their loved ones were found

murdered. They wanted to forget as best they could, they said. Some feared Anthony Sowell might walk away from the murders, perhaps on a mistrial. Imagine that—the man who had already pleaded not guilty by reason of insanity, then simply not guilty, freed after all this.

"Every time that I see him on television, it is just like watching the detectives walk back up on the porch again," said Joann Moore, Janice Webb's sister.

Eight of the families put together a petition that was presented to the office of Cuyahoga County Prosecutor Bill Mason. The only three families who didn't sign on were those of Tishana Culver, Nancy Cobbs, and Michelle Mason, each of whom sought the ultimate justice.

"I'm glad they getting ready to move this trial forward," said Culver's mother, Yvonne McNeill Williams. "It's been eighteen months and he's been sitting down there. They humanizing him. He took eleven lives, so why should his be saved?"

But the petition was a work of art, crafted with impactful words and as heartfelt as if it came from the lips of a, well, lawyer.

"We, the family members of the victims of the Imperial Avenue Murders, hereby petition to the Cuyahoga County Prosecutor's office to accept the guilty pleas of Anthony Sowell with a sentence of life imprisonment without the possibility of parole," the petition read, in part. "We do not want to endure a trial. We do not want to be witnesses to a media spectacle where our loved ones' lives and the details of the horrendous criminal acts inflicted upon them are spotlighted. The death penalty for Anthony Sowell is not necessary, or even desirable, in comparison to the grief we families will continue to suffer under the realities and uncertainties of the criminal justice system.

"We feel that our voices have not been heard as victims' families. A prolonged trial and re-enactment of Sowell's demented actions will create great distress on the families of the victims."

And when the press came calling, it was local attorney Jeffrey Friedman who went on the record, speaking for some of the families who had signed the petition.

Friedman had every reason to wish for a plea deal himself; he was representing eight families in lawsuits against the city over the Sowell case. A guilty plea would have made his job easier and also erased any possibility of a mistrial or of a jury finding of not guilty.

"As the media scrutiny got more intense and every place they went they were confronted, the families got more disillusioned," Friedman explained.

Indeed, defense attorneys John Parker and Rufus Sims asked that Anthony Sowell be allowed to plead guilty and waive all appeals. The police department was also asking that the court accept the guilty plea, a guarantee of life in prison. Their motivation was a post-conviction interview, where officers could learn about how Sowell had evaded them, how he'd captured his victims. These would be valuable learning tools, and the cops wanted the guilty plea accepted with the caveat that Sowell be required to tell them everything.

He was ready to do it.

But the county rejected the overture.

It surprised the defense; if the state were to lose this case on a technicality, the fallout would be severe.

"I didn't think the state should be taking such a costly risk," Sims says. "The state could take that deal and eliminate that risk. We have a decorated Marine here and this country doesn't have a record of putting decorated Marines to death."

But the state's position was that cases such as Sowell's were exactly why the state has the death penalty.

Rufus Sims was the man who got to know Anthony Sowell best. They shared a military background and bonded over both that and sports.

"He didn't trust me at all when we started," Sims says, recalling when he first met Sowell, in December 2009. "I couldn't get anything out of him. But pretty soon, we just talked sports; it was the best way to get to him."

They talked about football, basketball, baseball— anything that would fit in Sowell's comfort zone.

"My approach was 'we're going to discuss what he wants to discuss,'" Sims says. "We talked about the Browns, the Cavs."

Within a week, the two were talking about more serious things. They would do so for the next eighteen months.

At one point, Sims secured a photo of Sowell's graduating Marine class. When he showed him the picture, Sowell's face lit up like a new dime.

"Pick me out," he encouraged. Sims scanned the photo, but he couldn't find anyone who even looked close.

Sowell beamed when he pointed himself out.

Between the marksmanship accolades and Sowell's love for military operations, Sims thought, it was a good thing there had never been a shootout involved in the arrest between Sowell and the police.

"I don't know if the police could have won that one," Sims says.

Jury selection was the expected cattle call, initially beckoning 1,000 people, quickly paring that down to 300, and then using a computer program to randomly hone that to 200.

Those were the people who were invited to a clandestine meeting with Anthony Sowell on Friday, June 3, 2011.

It was an extra bit of caution on the part of Judge Ambrose, who greatly feared a mistrial. He carefully weighed every move he made, and this introduction of Sowell to jurors was an example of him going a little deeper on behalf of the defendant.

So in the afternoon that day, six jailers waited until Sowell had changed out of his jail uniform and put on a polo shirt and dress pants and escorted him to a room on the fourth floor of the Justice Center complex, where he walked in without handcuffs or leg irons. He was just a guy accused of murder, and everyone, including the prosecution and defense teams, looked at him.

"Hello," Sowell said when he was introduced. And that was all he had. It was awkward for everyone.

The thirty-six-page juror questionnaire asked the usual questions about views of crime, the death penalty, hobbies, vocations. It asked if they read true-crime books and, if so, asked them to name a couple of recently read titles.

In other places, the form was more direct.

"The facts of this case involve the alleged murders of eleven women as well as charges of rape and attempted rape involving three other women," it stated. "These incidents occurred from approximately 2007 to 2009, in the Mt. Pleasant neighborhood of Imperial Ave. and 123rd St., in Cleveland. Do you recall having read, seen or heard any media accounts reflecting these events?"

It listed 132 witnesses and asked if the jury was familiar with any of them, including Cleveland Mayor Frank Wilson. Some of them didn't know who he was.

By June 27, 2011, the jury was seated, though the middle-class group was hardly a jury of Sowell's peers. Among the twelve were a social worker, a student, two retirees, a grandfather, an insurance rep, and a UPS worker. Seven women and five men. On the morning of the first day, the group visited 12205 Imperial, which had been fenced off since the bodies were removed.

Little inside had changed since November 2009, although it was hard to tell how orderly the place may have been kept before the discovery of the bodies. Walls had been knocked out in the search for remains on the second and third floors, although the first floor was left pretty much intact.

The house itself "is not evidence, since conditions may have changed since the time of the events in this case," Judge Ambrose wrote in a court order. Jurors donned surgical masks to cover the smell of mildew and decay and also wore slip-on coverings for their shoes. They were guided by flashlights and walked over and around piles of men's and women's clothing, dishes crusted with food, empty beer cans, and empty bottles of Wild Irish Rose.

The tour, if done with the time and eye of a trained investigator, told the story of Sowell himself.

But much of what could be considered evidence had been carted away, of course. Although the jurors saw Sowell's bed, strewn with papers, they didn't see it as it was on October 29, 2009, when it was topped with a cheap beige velour blanket, pulled back to reveal a gray sheet that was stained with what looked like blood.

Although the jurors could note the small collection of CDs, including titles by Jay-Z and Ray Charles, as well as Abba and a collection of the band Chicago's hits, they missed the massive selection of movies on both VHS and DVD that had been taken as evidence. Among the titles: *Hannibal, Final Destination, Cradle 2 the Grave, Toy, Death on the Nile, The Medallion, The Replacement Killers*, a Looney Tunes collection, *Live Free or Die Hard, The Odyssey, Panic Room, In the Bedroom*, and *The Matrix*.

Sowell also had a porn DVD featuring Jake Steed, a

black performer whose films usually featured white females with Steed.

Some of the videos were stashed in suitcases, including a purple nylon case that was brimming with more pornography as well as a religious video from televangelist Jack Van Impe.

A nightstand, with a cheap single-CD boom box on it, no longer had several black-and-white photos—some dated and faded, some newer—of Sowell's sister Tressa and a number of small children.

On his dresser, a stereo-gear enthusiast would have noted a high-end Optonica stereo amp, made by Sharp in the late 1970s. Collectors still revere the defunct brand.

Some of the missing items, like the photos of his nieces and grandkids, would have perhaps evoked a more human perception of Sowell, although it's doubtful that, given his alleged deeds, anyone could connect the words *human* and *Sowell* at that time.

So, taking it all in, the jurors walked, looked, and said nothing.

The media tagged along, and it was a scene, with cop cars, three white county vans that ferried the jurors, and satellite trucks again lining the streets, like it was the body discovery all over again.

Prosecutor Pinkey Carr was also along to look through the house.

"It was surreal," she says. "I knew what happened in there, and I was just speechless. My homicide detectives talked to me and said, 'We've known you your entire professional career, and I don't think we've ever known you to be speechless.' It was just knowing what went on in that house that took me."

Judge Dick Ambrose came along as well, watching the jurors file into the house.

"I really don't want to have to do this over again," he confided to a cameraman from a local news station. His anxiety was palpable.

Square jawed and silver haired, Ambrose was used to pressure, though. He was a local hero from his days as a middle linebacker for the Cleveland Browns from 1975 to 1985, a standing that elevated him to sainthood in many eyes. When election time came around, Ambrose used a photo of himself on his reelection website, smiling, wearing his robe, with the Cleveland Browns Stadium behind him.

After his graduation from law school in 1987, he joined a local firm and spent seventeen years in private practice as a business employment law specialist.

He was appointed to the bench in 2004 by then Ohio governor Bob Taft, and in October, he ran to be elected. He used his former celebrity candidly, going with a football theme and Browns colors for his campaign literature. Postcards he handed out at events showed a photo of him in his Browns uniform on the front and the 2004 Browns schedule on the back.

His defeat in that election didn't keep him off the bench, though; he was appointed again by Taft in January 2005, and this time he kept the office.

Area politicos liked Ambrose. He was a friendly man as well as being considered an earnest judge. But he was also sensitive to the notion among some that he was a jock who'd been elected on the merits of his gridiron prowess, not his legal expertise.

"He works harder because of that," says one local political observer. "Ambrose was a very popular football player, and the things he does now draw more attention. So he always seems to be as good as he can be, and that's usually very good."

Ambrose's cases ran the gamut, from small stuff like prostitution rings and burglary to murder. He upheld the death-penalty recommendation of a jury in 2005 in the case of Delano Hale Jr., who shot a man to death in a Cleveland motel room.

The Ohio Supreme Court upheld a challenge to procedural errors in Ambrose's court.

In other words, Ambrose had no reservations about the death penalty.

But as a Republican in a Democratic stronghold, Ambrose was also no straight-ticket partisan; when the Ohio legislature attempted to loosen the restrictions on criminal-record expungement for prisoners who had served their time, Ambrose took up the cause.

Now, at fifty-eight, he was presiding over a murder trial that he knew would magnify any judicial fumble. Among his defense arsenal: he issued a gag order limiting attorney comment outside court and putting his office off-limits to reporters.

\* \* \*

"You are about to begin a rather disturbing journey," assistant Prosecutor Richard Bombik told the jury. "It will be burned into your memory for as long as you live."

It was 2 P.M. on Monday, June 27, 2011, and the jurors were fed and watered after their trip through the Sowell house. Security was heavy, both for the safety of others from Sowell, whose crimes were unspeakably violent, and to protect Sowell from any family member whose rage simply couldn't be quelled.

Anthony Sowell sat between his attorneys, John Parker and Rufus Sims, wearing a white sweater and black pants. He also wore a blank expression, as he would for much of the four-week trial.

"There are 14 main victims in this indictment," Bombik continued. "Eleven that are dead and three who lived to talk about it. Everything that happened in this case happened in the house you visited today, 12205 Imperial. It begins and ends with this house."

At that, a picture of the house flashed on a large screen in front of the jurors.

"It's an old house, and it's been the Sowell household for many many years. . . . It goes way back."

Bombik went through the history of the house and the Sowell family, starting with John Sowell. He noted that Segerna Sowell had died on December 19, 2009, after a long illness. But before she did, she lived with her stepson for a while. Bombik described the living quarters upstairs.

Bombik referred to Sowell's relationship with Lori Frazier as "very important."

"Miss Frazier would spend the better part of the next two years, 2006 and 2007, living with Anthony Sowell," he said. "I think the evidence is going to show at the beginning of this relationship, she had a drug problem, which eventually would go over to Anthony Sowell. It was an up-and-down relationship, but it was a relationship that was very important to Anthony Sowell, very important. But like many other relationships in life, this did not work out and she moved out of this house sometime in 2007. She would occasionally maintain contact with him. Evidence will show shortly after she moved out, things began to happen."

Bombik narrated each victim's disappearance, showing a collage of photos of the victims on the screen. They all had drug problems, he acknowledged.

Then he hinted at a surprise, perhaps the only true surprise of the trial.

Bombik mentioned a young lady named Vanessa Gay, whom few in the room or among the media had heard of. He told of how, like other women, Vanessa had gone up to Sowell's room in September 2008 to get high.

"Vanessa who will come in here and testify that sometime either in September or August 2008, she'll talk about how she came across and met Anthony Sowell on the streets, and he invited her to celebrate his birthday with her. Mr. Sowell's birthday is August 19, that will be a clear fact if in fact he wanted to celebrate his birthday with her it would be on or around August 19, 2008. And she, too, went over, she will testify, that she went over to his house with the expectation of getting high with Mr. Sowell and made it up to the third floor of the house, his living quarters where she will testify he attacked her. And you will hear the details of that in due time. Miss Gay likewise had brushes with the law and substance abuse problems. She will recall being let go by Mr. Sowell but before being let go she will relate to you an observation she made in the other room that will be somewhat disturbing."

As he wound down an hour of opening, Bombik tersely read a roll call of the victims and how they died.

"Tonia Carmichael, electric cord around neck, naked. Diane Turner, homicidal violence . . ."

Sowell listened and looked at the pictures of the deceased as they were put up on the screen.

Bombik finished with a flourish. He stopped, creased his brow for the sixtieth time in an hour, and looked at the floor.

"On Saturday October 31, a citizen saw Sowell. . . . They got him as he was walking down the street, this alleged killer disguised as a normal human being on Halloween."

He ended: "I look forward to bringing Anthony Sowell to justice. And I also look forward to bringing justice to Anthony Sowell."

John Parker had little to offer visually.

While Bombik was dressed in a flattering dark suit and

wore a sharp, dark blue tie and was well-coiffed, Parker was not. He looked a bit disheveled, clad in an ill-fitting suit and a light silver tie. He did exactly what he should do, though, speaking about the witnesses and the notion that the rapes and the kidnappings are different from murder.

"You'll hear from them from the witness stand what happened to each and every one of them as they tell it," Parker said. "These are two separate categories, cases that the state has decided to bring together—as you heard early on there are 85 cases charges as relates to homicide victims and charges as relates to the other women. It's critical for you to understand and you will find throughout this trial with respect to the homicides that there are six crimes charged to Mr. Sowell. There are no rapes, there are no attempted rapes, there are no sex crimes charged against him as it relates to the homicide victims. You will also find out as it relates to the homicide victims that there are no eyewitnesses, there are no fingerprints, there's no evidence linking Mr. Sowell to the homicides. . . . There is not significant forensic evidence linking Mr. Sowell to the homicides."

Parker, his glasses occasionally sliding awkwardly down his sweaty nose, continued.

"I think you will also find at the end of this case that the manner in which the crime scene was handled, the house, the backyard, you will find the crime scene was handled very poorly, and that may have impact—or it may not have, that's up to you."

He tried to convey the notion that the victims were

subject to dubious honesty, without outright saying that drug users' characters were not always stellar.

"These women had many problems you will hear about, problems with substance abuse, with health issues. You will have to determine if what they tell you is truthful and if you find them to be truthful, which part of their testimony is truth."

He ended with a request.

"Please be patient, listen to the evidence," Parker said.

At the defense table, a bottle of 5-hour Energy drink sat before Rufus Sims. Every day around 3 P.M., he would down a bottle. These were fifteen-hour days he was pulling, arriving at the office at 6 A.M. some days and not getting home until 9 or 9:30 in the evening.

The state came with a full blast of witnesses that tugged heartstrings and told of a street lifestyle that most people never hear of, a life of mental evaluations and jail time and courtrooms and drugs. Relatives of the deceased told heartbreaking stories of their loved ones, of taking DNA to an appointed place to find out if their missing daughter or mother was among the bodies of the murdered women found on Imperial.

Anthony Sowell's beloved ex-girlfriend Lori Frazier answered questions in her smoky voice, talking of meeting Sowell and the last time she saw him, when he came to see her at Charley's Grilled Subs.

"He just popped up and asked why I didn't remember his birthday," she said. Lori talked about her friend Crystal Dozier, whom she had known since elementary school. They had gotten high together as they grew up, although she said she never took Crystal to the Sowell house.

"When was the last time you saw her?" Pinkey Carr asked.

"A place on Griffin," Lori said. "It was all in the same neighborhood, but I don't remember the date. It was warm out."

She also told of "somebody" digging a hole in the backyard of the house on Imperial after she'd moved out and was coming back for periodic visits. She said Sowell told her it was because a toilet had backed up. It was a plumbing thing, she figured.

John Parker got the big stuff out in the open right away on his cross-examination.

Lori was staying with her mother, Eleanor, when she met Sowell. "Eleanor's sister is married to the Mayor of Cleveland," Parker noted.

"What's that got to do with anything?" Lori spat.

He looked at a report in his hand and remarked that she had lost custody of her four kids at some point during the years before she met Sowell. He asked her why.

"Because I was getting high on the streets," she said indignantly.

"Where did you get the drugs?" he asked.

"Somebody gave 'em to me," she said. "People, around."

She sat, steaming, as Parker silently read a bit more and prepared another question.

"What's my getting high got to do with this?" she said, her voice raising.

Parker pushed it, getting her angrier. He asked about her hospitalization for mental issues in 2002.

"Did you try to harm yourself?" he asked, knowing it was in the report.

"I don't know, I don't remember," Lori said, now turning in her chair and looking away from him.

"You got treatment, they gave you drugs to take for it," Parker said.

"I took crack, that's what I needed," Lori said, in full anger.

Parker now read aloud from the report, noting a diagnosis of a psychotic disorder and outpatient mental-health care. She was prescribed Paxil, a potent antidepressant, but didn't take it.

"It made me jittery," she said, failing to grasp that crack would, to most people, be the most potent inducer of jitters imaginable.

Parker had established one thing early, something that would remain through the four weeks of the trial; almost every one of the women from the street put up by the state had serious credibility issues.

It was all he could do, though. The bodies were still just as dead.


The next day came the surprise.

A twenty-seven-year-old woman named Vanessa Gay

took the stand, a pleasant-looking woman who lived on Broadway, about four miles from Imperial.

As Bombik gently questioned her, Vanessa told of her husband and three children and her inability to control her drug habit, which had begun in 2006.

"The drugs led me to the streets, specifically the Mount Pleasant neighborhood," she said, an area that included Imperial.

Bombik guided her verbally, as Vanessa was already beginning to sniffle and tear up.

Still, she soldiered on.

She told how, in September 2008, "my life was worse than it had ever been."

"Sometime in September 2008, did you have occasion to be looking to get high?" Bombik asked.

Yes, she said. "It was around 10, or 10:30 at night. I was on foot, and I was near 140th Avenue and Kinsman on the same side as Key Bank, thinking what I was going to do. I wasn't high and I didn't get high that day and I was contemplating whether I was going to go in or stay out."

A man walked by her as she stood still. He was talking on his cell phone and telling someone that it was his birthday, she said.

When Bombik asked her if that man was in the courtroom, Vanessa broke into tears again.

"He's over there," she said, pointing to Sowell, sitting in a pressed sweater and looking on passively.

On that night, Vanessa said, he was telling whomever

he was talking to that he had no one to celebrate his birthday with, "and I said, 'I celebrate birthdays, so happy birthday.'"

The two began to talk and walk, and Sowell introduced himself and in passing told her he had some crack and some alcohol and asked her to celebrate his birthday with him.

"I said 'ok," Vanessa testified. As they walked the few blocks to Imperial, they talked about cooking and he told her of his time in the military, "and it was a pleasant conversation about just cooking, who was the best cook and things like that."

They arrived at the house, she said, and Sowell pointed out the sign on the porch railing that read "The Sowells," black with red lettering.

He had some weed, some wine—"E and J," she said, slang for Ernest and Julio Gallo, which made the popular street wine, Night Train—and told her that he had "a 50," a $50 chunk of crack, in his hand, which was balled up.

"He told me we were going up to the third floor," Vanessa said. As she spoke, her voice careened all over the emotional map. The courtroom was riveted. Everyone had known about the alleged atrocities, but no one had heard of how any of them went down, until now.

They went up the stairs to the third floor, and "it was dark in there and it was like stale, just musty, stinky, dirty, it was like dark and gloomy, you could feel the gloom."

Vanessa described the upstairs apartment in precise

detail, down to the miniature refrigerator and the curtains covering the window in his bedroom, which overlooked the back wall of Ray's Sausage.

He produced the rock and asked if she had a stem—a kind of pipe used to smoke crack.

"I handed it to him," Vanessa said, "and he turned around and put something in it . . . and [lit] it, and [I] could see the smoke come up. After he took a hit, he turned around and punched me in the face and said 'bitch take your clothes off.' He told me if I didn't do what he said to a tee, he was going to throw me in the closet and forget about me."

And now, on the stand, with what seemed like the whole world watching, Vanessa Gay began to cry uncontrollably.

Bombik stood patiently. Sowell sat stone-faced and watched her cry.

Vanessa composed herself and went on.

"He went into a rant about his ex-girlfriend and how crack made her and how he was going get those women back who did him wrong when he smoked crack."

"He said, 'you don't deserve what I'm about to do to you' and it was all bad after that," Vanessa said. Sowell raped her repeatedly, she said. He kept talking about how he was wronged by other women. He hit her again. She kept agreeing with him.

Courtrooms can be uncomfortable places, and the horrors that people inflict on each other are often bared there. But no one was prepared for this.

Vanessa's sobs muddled parts of her story, but there

was no one who did not believe it. Even under the glare of incandescent lights and with the company of dozens of people, those watching could feel her aloneness in telling this story.

Then it got worse.

The night faded into daylight, and Vanessa asked if she could use the bathroom, which was located just one door down from the bedroom to the right.

Sowell told her where it was, and she got up and walked out the bedroom door. She cast a glance into the bedroom across the hall as she did so. It was dark when they had walked down the hall before, but now, the morning light was filtering in.

And in that room across the hall, she saw a body wrapped in plastic. And in the courtroom, Vanessa came apart, crying and blurting out, "The plastic was pulled up and there was . . . It looked like it was a body. It looked like there was no head on it. It was propped up, sitting on the floor."

Everything in the courtroom stopped as she cried in shaking sobs, tears wetting her powder-blue blouse. It took a full minute before Vanessa could compose herself again.

She said Sowell was behind her and she knew she couldn't react. And she couldn't believe her eyes.

"I kept thinking to myself, 'I couldn't have possibly seen that,'" she said. "'This can't be real.' But I knew what I saw."

They went back to the bedroom, and Sowell was worried she would go to the police over the rape.

"He said, 'you're gonna tell, I know you're gonna tell.'

And I said I am not gonna tell," Vanessa said. "I was saying, 'what is there to tell?'"

He let her go with a promise that she would come back in a few days, when he got paid. She said yes. She walked out of 12205 Imperial alive.

Vanessa stayed at a friend's house and slept for three days, then called the police.

They told her they couldn't take a report over the phone; she had to come in.

"I didn't know who to turn to, I felt less than human already," Vanessa said. She'd had enough experiences being hassled by the cops.

"I felt horrible going to the police," she said. "I had no confidence in the police, none, none. They failed me before."

She never reported it.

A year later, she recognized Sowell's picture in the newspaper as bodies were being discovered in the house.

After the bomb that was Vanessa Gay's testimony, there was no future for the defense of Anthony Sowell. It was three days in, and by the tenth witness, Sowell was guilty in almost everyone's eyes.

Parker barely even tried to impugn her. He saved that for later, when it would be too late.


A parade of family members and the other survivors, including Gladys Wade and Latundra Billups, meshed with the faceless officials from the coroner's office, cops, and so-called experts to create a legal spiderweb from which Anthony Sowell could never escape. Sixty-two witnesses told of the horrendous trail of death and violence he had left.

The defense, with a price tag now reaching $600,000, lay down. It didn't call a single witness, deflated by the intensity of the victims and the families of the deceased.

Parker and Sims now simply sought to keep their client alive.

Sowell's only hope was a mistrial or a sadly misguided jury, and neither appeared to be in the cards.

There were a few lighter moments in the trial, however, when even Sowell broke from his blankness and smiled.

His stepgrandmother, Virginia Oliver, took the stand early in the trial. The eighty-nine-year-old woman, Segerna's mother, was at the point in her life where she had no filters on what she said.

Virginia was brittle and endearing. When assistant prosecutor Pinkey Carr flashed a picture of Segerna on the video screen, Virginia beamed and said, "That's my baby."

She described Segerna's health woes as her life wound to a close, with seven operations, and told of how Sowell had helped his stepmother.

"And do you see Anthony here today?" Pinkey asked in a motherly voice.

Sowell stood up halfway as she looked at him with a wide smile.

"Hi Anthony," she said brightly. He returned her smile and waved.

But smiles were brief.

When the two legal teams would break from the script, when the jury and onlookers were out of the courtroom, there would be some lightness, a bit of kidding.

"There were times during the trial when defense lawyers and I would laugh about something," says Carr. "And Sowell would laugh and I would think 'why are you laughing? This is not funny for you, you're the whole reason we're going through this.' And I would immediately stop laughing."

Levity was in short supply.

Anthony Sowell was a killer from the outset.

Vanessa Gay sealed the deal in that first week. The rest was all window dressing.

Bombik came out with closing remarks for the prosecution first. Using a PowerPoint presentation to give his delivery some graphic appeal, he stressed, as he had in his opening remarks, the house on Imperial.

He said the house is "condemned forever."

"The question that begs for an answer is who lives here?" Bombik said. "And the answer to that question is Anthony Sowell. Make no doubt about it."

He continued. "This is not complicated. Don't make it complicated. The evidence in this case is overwhelming. It is enormous. Label him for what he is, a serial killer."

Bombik added that it takes three to five minutes of intense pressure to snuff out a life via strangulation, and "that is a long, long time. That is a blueprint of prior calculation and design if ever there was one, because you can stop. But he was on a hell-bent mission to cause their deaths."

The PowerPoint presentation showed photos of the victims, their underwear, their jewelry, and the ligatures that were used in some cases to snuff out their lives.

The photos of the victims included them alive, smiling, and vibrant, as well as their decomposed remains.

Bombik also noted that most of the women were tied up, naked from the waist down, and wrapped in garbage bags or buried in shallow graves in the backyard of the Imperial house.

He made a last plea for death as he ended his address. If the jury opts for prison, "where's the punishment? You're sending him home to a place where he does well."

Carr then came in with a likewise strong delivery, with a dramatic flair.

Clad in a black skirt and blouse, her long, dark hair artfully tousled, Carr summarized the testimony from the survivors. If that wasn't enough to make you believe them, she said, "look at the exhibits. Who can make this stuff up?"

"Look at her neck," Carr said, indicating a photo of Gladys Wade's injuries to the jury. "What, did she do this herself? Oh no, this has Tony written all over it. Tony likes to choke a girl." She laid the photo down on the lectern. "What about Latundra? Is she lying too?"

For sarcastic drama, the prosecutor tossed an aside.

"He's a choker," she said, drawing it out in two long syllables, as *choke-er*.

"When you strangle somebody, it's personal," she

continued. "Personal. You've got to get up close to a person . . . Tony was so close to these girls he could smell the fear."

To emphasize her point, Carr walked up behind the state's law clerk, Chris Schroeder, and wrapped her forearm around his neck.

"What about the girls he choked from the front? He had to be in their face, just sucked the life out of them."

"Three to five minutes," she said, restating Bombik's point of how long it takes to exterminate a life through strangulation. "Who does that?"

"He did it because he's evil. He did it because he's a serial killer," Carr said. "He did it."

"I know everybody said he's a good guy. He helped out everyone, he I guess ran an all night cemetery too. 'Tony, you think I can put this body in your basement?' Because he was a nice guy."

Carr slowly held up a picture of each of the eleven women whose bodies had been found in and around the house on Imperial.

"Find him guilty of each and every count. Do justice," she said softly.

Defense Attorney John Parker came to his final arguments with less flair but just as much candor.

Parker asked jurors to consider the witnesses, singling out Vanessa Gay's testimony that she saw a headless body in Sowell's third-floor dwelling.

"She has a history of drug abuse and mental illness. She hears and sees things that aren't there," Parker said.

He also noted that there was no DNA that tied Sowell to the murders—and he was correct.

"To prove who strangled these women, wouldn't you want to test the ligatures? Just one of them? This man, who is an honorably discharged U.S. Marine, deserves better . . . But the state didn't even try."

On Friday, July 22, 2011, after three days of deliberation, the jury announced it had reached a verdict.

Wearing a gray polo shirt, glasses, and clean-cut goatee, Anthony Sowell first stood and then sat, defiant and stoic, when the verdict was read aloud. It took an hour, given the multiple counts. The jury found him guilty on eighty-four of eighty-five counts; he slid on the aggravated robbery count.

When it was over, Sowell yawned.

A team of bailiffs surrounded him quickly. As the lawyers milled about and the gallery stood to watch, to soak in the judicial victory, Sowell had one parting gesture: as he left, he lifted his manacled hands in the air above him, as if in some victory that no one else could understand, as Parker and Sims looked on in surprise. It was the first time in the past month that Sowell had shown his soul.

# CHAPTER 16

I truly am sorry from the bottom of my heart.
This is not typical of me.

**—ANTHONY SOWELL**

There was one last element to the proceedings that finished Anthony Sowell's fate. Would he live his natural life out in a prison, or would he be put to death by the state?

The last Cuyahoga County jury to recommend death was in 2007, when a man named Charles Maxwell was convicted of killing his ex-girlfriend, shooting her twice while her young daughter looked on. It was the night before the little girl's fourth birthday.

On Monday, August 1, 2011, the mitigation part of the sentencing began. Under Ohio law, a defendant is entitled to these actions in order to determine if capital punishment is warranted. It is a method of precaution before deciding on the ultimate punishment.

A parade of social workers was scheduled by the defense. They called Roosevelt Lloyd, Sowell's former cell mate throughout the 1990s in the Ohio correctional system.

Lloyd, who was released in 2009, said that when Sowell was released, in 2005, staffers hugged him good-bye, hardly protocol in the hardened prison world.

On the stand, Lloyd came across as humble, but his message was a jumbled mess of regret and support for a man who had absolutely zero support among the audience.

"Anthony Sowell, I don't appreciate what he did," Lloyd said. "You know what he did as wrong. Very wrong. I mean, very wrong. What you all see of Anthony Sowell today is what he done for that period. But what you don't see or understand about him, Anthony Sowell, is before he got like that. He's a nice, loving, caring person. Now what could have triggered this event here today, I don't know. But what I do know is that the people who love him . . . some of them don't even want their names mentioned. These are the people that I know that love him. And I just couldn't see myself turning my back on him. Because that man you see right over there, I love him like a brother. Regardless of what he done, he deserve not to die. . . . killing him ain't going to bring nobody back. He's a disturbed young man. I didn't know how disturbed until this happened. But if you knew him 15 years ago, you would have loved him like everybody else. I'm going to ask this court, ask the judge, ask the jury, have mercy on him. Cause we all do bad things in life, we all do bad things. He's not going anywhere. His life is over."

As Lloyd made his plea in court, Sowell teared up

unashamedly, and he mouthed the words, "No way" as he shook his head no.

But the biggest of all witnesses took the stand Monday, August 8, when Sowell himself took the stand on his own behalf. Under the law, he could not be cross-examined, since he had already been found guilty.

It was the first time the world would listen to Sowell, aside from the police-interrogation videos that the jurors had been shown during the trial.

Sowell wore a black polo shirt and black slacks and looked every bit the gentleman.

He slumped his shoulders meekly on the stand, but he listened carefully as defense attorney John Parker asked him scripted questions about his life.

Parker's questions quickly got to a point—that Sowell had been sexually abused by a cousin when he was six or seven years old.

He spoke of growing up in a house with "a lot of sexual activity" among the children, much of it forced on the younger kids by the older ones.

Jurors recalled that Sowell was accused by one of his nieces of having raped her repeatedly when he was a teen-ager. Now, it was Sowell who was telling of sexual abuse.

He shied away from much of it, though, later saying that he just couldn't get himself to talk about the abuse despite the probing of Parker.

"I can't talk about it so freely in front of strangers like that," Sowell says.

"It was like a war in there," Sowell said, speaking of

his house as he grew up. It was the first time most everyone, aside from the defense team, had heard Sowell speak anything more than two or three words at a time, and the courtroom was riveted.

Sowell spoke with a Southern accent, vastly different than the Southern-inflected midwestern accent so many people in his neighborhood carried with them.

The word *kids* was pronounced "kee-ids" and *on* became "own."

Hoping to make Sowell at least a pinch sympathetic, Parker asked him about his school days, about his time in the Marines, and his marriage to Kim Yvette Lawson. Sowell's replies were a tortured rendering of his emotional state.

If it had been anyone else, it would have evoked great sympathy, but jurors listened and looked in studied fascination, as if a being from another planet was telling a fictional tale.

He told of his incarceration from 1990 to 2005, which the jury was hearing of for the first time; as was typical, priors had been ruled off-limits during the trial.

Sowell also told the jury about his heart attack in 2007, losing his job at Custom Rubber, and the depression that took him over in its wake.

Then, in wrapping up, Parker asked Sowell if he had anything to say to the families of the victims.

"Well, all I can say is I'm sorry. I know that it might not sound that much but I truly am sorry from the bottom of my heart. This is not typical of me. I don't know what happened. I can't explain it. Well, I know it's not a lot but that's all I can give."

Sims never thought twice about the wisdom of putting Sowell on the stand.

"You never know what you're going to get when he gets up there," Sims says. "You just hope he doesn't go off. He probably thought he did a good job. And I think that some people, no matter what you say to threaten them, are only going to go so far to apologize."

Almost across the board, Sowell failed miserably in his opportunity to makes things better. It's not as if words could fix this one, anyway.

The mitigation phase ended with Sowell's testimony, and the jury was sent home. On Wednesday, August 10, 2011, the jurors returned with a verdict, after deliberating for seven hours. They decided that Anthony Sowell should receive the death penalty.

Sowell was again led off by bailiffs.

The only thing left was for Judge Ambrose to sign off. It was a long process for a short end. Everyone knew what the judge would do.

After two months of courtroom proceedings, Judge Ambrose sat down to finish the case. Before he began, he asked the victims who chose to address the court to do so with "decorum" and again thanked the jury.

Ambrose read back the guilty counts in a droning voice, as well as he could manage with the material.

Sowell, now looking more like a prisoner in his orange

jailhouse jumpsuit, sat at the defense table with his eyes closed. He refused to look up or acknowledge anyone or anything.

Before announcing his own decision, Ambrose asked Sowell if he had anything to say.

"Mr. Sowell you have the right to elocution or the right to make a statement here before the court before the court proceeds any further. Do you wish to make a statement to the court, Mr. Sowell?"

Sowell sat, head slightly turned down, eyes closed as if asleep. Silence.

"I don't believe he wishes to speak," defense attorney John Parker said.

"He's not going to make any verbal response to that?" Ambrose said, somewhat taken aback.

"No," Parker said, standing.

"All right then, Mr. Sowell, I'm proceeding on the basis that you do not wish to make a statement," Ambrose said. "You've been advised that you have the opportunity; you chose to remain silent when the court offered you that opportunity."

Ambrose continued, "It is necessary for me to review with the defendant his registration requirements again because there are several rape charges here and also sexual motivation specifications for which the jury has found the defendant guilty of. I have to review with him the requirements as a tier III sex offender before we can go any further."

Ambrose read the long list of reporting obligations for a sex offender. It was ridiculous—Sowell was never going to be free again, and the requirements applied only to a free man. But Ambrose pushed ahead. Sowell kept his eyes closed, not moving.

When the judge finished and asked Sowell to sign the form stating that he understood the registration requirements, Sowell continued to simply sit, eyes closed, head bowed. It was a long five seconds of silence.

"I don't think he's going to sign this," Parker said, pulling the form close to sign on behalf of his client.

Ambrose showed no inclination to make things lively; indeed, his straight-ahead legalese made lids heavy, until several others joined Sowell in the eyes-closed, head-down pose.

Ambrose read his own review, naming the specialists who showed what proved Sowell's guilt.

"The court, having gone through its independent analysis, has accepted the jury's verdicts," Ambrose said.

Ambrose then addressed Sowell, who sat at the defense table with his eyes still closed.

"If you did feel bad, then I would have some hope for you," Ambrose said, looking at the lethargic Sowell. "Not for your physical well-being here on earth, because that's been decided in court—but for your eternal well-being."

Ambrose set an execution date of October 29, 2012, the third anniversary of the discovery of the first bodies on Imperial, though the reality was that it would probably be decades before the execution.

The family members berated him, poured out their pure grief.

The most piercing, heartrending statement came from

Donald Smith, the father of victim Kim Smith. He had cried when he testified, and he wept now.

"He took my heart, my life," Donald said. "And I might as well die, too, because he killed a part of me."

Others vented their hatred for Anthony Sowell in statements that dripped with agony.

"In my opinion you're going to hell for your actions," Donnita Carmichael said. "Anthony you are an animal and hell awaits your arrival. I won't stand up here and tell you that I'm not bitter, because I am. I'll never forgive you."

Sowell kept his eyes closed. Three bailiffs stood behind him. When the proceeding was over, Sowell rose wearily and was taken back to his cell. He looked bored.

The day after the verdict, Pinkey Carr took the day off. And she skipped the gym.

"I watched TV, *Judge Mathis*," Carr says. "It was a relaxing day; I stayed in the house. I was grateful and thankful for the experience."

She was still angry about Sowell's lackluster apology on the stand, his "this is not typical of me" defense.

"When I was sitting there listening to that, I was pissed," Carr says. "My mouth was wide open, Rick and I were sitting next to each other. When Sowell said, 'That's all I can give,' well, I was surprised his lawyers didn't prepare him better."

Sims was not surprised. He says he got to know Anthony Sowell "better than anyone."

"You don't know what you're going to get when he goes up there," Sims says. "Some people no matter what you say, even if you threaten them, they are only going to go so far to apologize. He probably thought he did a good job that day. But people want to see the emotion, and he didn't have that."

In November, Carr was elected as a judge for the Cleveland Municipal Court, defeating an incumbent appointee.

On August 30, Sowell was again in the courtroom of Judge Ambrose, as Parker had filed a motion for a new trial based on what he claimed was juror misconduct.

After delivering the verdict, the jury made a highly unusual move; as a group, it called a press conference to address the media.

In particular, the jury foreman, a woman of around thirty-five, went on camera and dropped two bombs that will no doubt provide years of legal wrangling over the impartiality of the jury and the Constitutional rights of Anthony Sowell.

The woman told reporters that during the jury's tour of the house on Imperial Avenue, she became "overwhelmed." She said she had to take a second to get it together before completing the tour.

"I think [Sowell] made a lot of eye contact when it was to his benefit," she added. "And it personally offended me because he even winked at me once. What was that about? Why are you winking? This is serious here, your life is on the line, why are you winking?"

* * *

Sims and Parker subpoenaed a tape of her comments and asked Judge Ambrose to declare a mistrial. It was quickly denied.

It was Sowell's attitude that again shocked when he was brought back into the courtroom for the hearing.

"Don't bring me back here for that bullshit," he complained to the bailiffs. "I was sleeping nicely."

The jurors never reconciled one thing: the smell that was widely but randomly discussed, as if it was just assumed that the smell was the rotting corpses of Sowell's victims.

Frazier said that she became aware of an odd smell in early 2006. The Pompeys, who lived on the second floor with their infant daughter at the time, also said they smelled something like decay.

It wasn't until June of 2007 that the city received a complaint and sent someone out to look into the odor and ordered Ray Cash Jr. to spend $20,000 on cleaning things up, thinking that would end it. It didn't.

So what was it that was stinking in 2006, when the women didn't start disappearing until May 2007, when Crystal Dozier was last seen?

There are varying accounts of the odor that wafted through the Imperial Avenue area. Some claimed it had been part of the environment for years, even prior to Sowell's arrival in 2005.

Eobbie Dancy, Amelda Hunter's son, says he worked

at Ray's Sausage during the summer of 2005—preceding Sowell's arrival to the neighborhood—and there was a smell then.

"It turned out to be a skunk," Dancy says.

When Richard Bombik delivered his masterful, one-hour opening statement, he didn't mention the smell that had been in so many news reports.

Several trial witnesses, such as the Pompeys and Raymond Cash, mentioned the smell. But the odor was never a factor in the conviction of Sowell.

There is little doubt that the decomposing bodies emitted a bad smell. Coroner's office workers had to wear masks when they began gathering up the remains at the house on Imperial.

But what was it that Lori Frazier smelled in 2006? Were there other bodies that Sowell had stashed before her arrival, during that two or three months that Sowell and Segerna lived there on the first floor? The questions create a one-year window of wonder; surely there were other women going missing in that time, perhaps women who were never recovered. The questions still stand out there, wavering, wafting.

On September 14, 2011, Sowell left the Cuyahoga County Jail, where he had been for nearly two years. He first went to the Lorain County Jail for processing; then, on September 15, he went to the Ohio State Penitentiary in Youngstown, Ohio. He was assigned a one-man cell on death row, awaiting the day he would be moved to

Lucasville, to spend the night before his execution. As of September 30, 2011, there were 148 inmates awaiting execution. Some had been there since 1983.

Anthony Sowell most likely has a long time to wait.

# AUTHOR'S NOTE

As I was writing this book, the chapters hit me like a chest thump, one tragic story after another, all gathered together by this guy who had become a real presence to me, Anthony Sowell.

There is an order to this story, and it's composed of women going missing and women being violently attacked. I tended to grab off chunks that were stories and write them, then assembling all in a cut-and-paste fashion.

I finished the piece on the Gladys Wade case before I did that of Tonia Carmichael, even though, technically, Carmichael went missing shortly before Gladys had her encounter with Anthony Sowell.

There were so many of these encounters that sometimes it became a confusing timeline. It was put together like a puzzle, and I hope it works for you.

I read it back, and it brings home the thudding ferocity and rapid-fire intensity of these incredibly violent incursions and the hard lives of the victims. One after another, women went missing. And each had a story that was almost unbelievable in its misfortune, heartbreak, calamity—name that tortured element.

One evening I watched the brief, edited video of Donald Smith, father of victim Kim Smith, testifying at Sowell's trial, and I fought the urge to call him, at 11 P.M. on a weeknight, just to let him know he wasn't alone in his grief. These kinds of things happen a lot when I write this material, which may mean I'm not cut out for it. Seems that the heavyweights can just cruise through it. I can't. I struggle with it; I dream about it; I stare into space.

As the individual vignettes were completed, I would write next to each name *DONE* in caps to let me know I had given that victim's story. It was weirdly satisfying, even though I knew that subsequent phone calls and visits with survivors would yield more and give each person more importance and humanity. When I read news accounts of Diane Turner's sad life and looked through her numerous arrests for drugs, I found myself deep in her pathological need for drugs, trying to wrap my head around it.

The same week I wrote of Turner's saga, a friend of mine died of a heroin overdose. I had seen him ten days previously, and we had a great visit, laughing and talking about mutual friends and the neighborhood and the city we both lived in, Lansing, Michigan. Then he was dead. Just like that. He didn't live like Diane Turner, who fought all her life just to score. He just bought some dope, shot it up, and it all stopped.

I was very depressed about the whole thing and spent part of each day in mourning. Then, at night, I would again sit down to write this book. Cue darkness. Somehow, Diane made sense to me. A craving is a craving, and we all do what it takes to get by.

Then there was the frustration I felt for the families trying to navigate a system that seems skewed against anyone having to deal with it.

Frequently, I would try to refer to the state of Ohio's corrections department website for assistance in tracking an offender, perhaps to see if he or she was now in state custody. The site was almost always out of commission, and I realized that the state had little interest in helping people who are trying to find out the status of someone, perhaps a victim wanting to make sure an offender isn't running free.

It was the same thing with the prison's system for setting up a phone account so one may have phone contact with a prisoner. The bureaucracy was stifling, and I can imagine someone unaccustomed to navigating such a thing being overwhelmed by the frustration. The burden is already heavy; the system makes it worse.

It really shouldn't be that way, but this is how the families of criminals are treated, as if it were their fault the crime happened.

It comes back to the lackadaisical and inept responses that the Cleveland Police Department gave the families of these victims. The attitude is one of great dehumanization and disdain for a large part of the public that pays for its existence.

At the very least, some simple training is in order. These officers are smart to put on their game face at the same time they put on their uniforms, because civilized traits like empathy and helpfulness are often seen as signs of weakness on the street. But like anyone else, you have to adapt to circumstances. Someone reporting a missing person is not an immediate threat.

The department has an incredibly burdensome job in handling both society's most unfortunate as well as our most pathological and evil.

And the numbers provided by the police department tell a compelling story. In 2009, the year Sowell was apprehended, the Cleveland police took 2,232 missing-persons reports, and 2,227 were found, returned, or otherwise accounted for. Most frequently, those reported missing are teenagers, and around 83 percent are black.

In Sowell's case, one has to remember that police said only three of the eleven victims were actually reported missing—Tonia Carmichael, Janice Webb, and Michelle Mason—although some other families claimed they filed reports, when cops say they didn't, or that their claims were dismissed.

Police often decline to take a report if there is not some evidence that a missing-person's life is endangered. And that's not just Cleveland police. And who's to say, in their panic and grief, that the family members trying to explain their concern did an effective job?

A month after the Sowell case broke, Cleveland Mayor Frank Jackson established a three-person panel to study the way the police handle sexual assaults and missing-person cases.

So began the roundabout, a blur of surveys and white papers that mean nothing to the cop on the street, who is dealing with life and death and horrors that most people watch on their flat-screen TVs as a form of entertainment on sanitized shows like *Cops.*

Within months, the panel released a report with twenty-six recommendations. Among them was the creation of a missing-persons unit.

In April 2011, the city hired Wilson Research Strategies, now known as WPA Opinion Research, to embark on a study that includes an audit of detectives' caseloads, a quality-assurance investigation, and a survey of the community's perception of police.

This is how a huge bureaucracy handles a crisis; WPA Opinion Research is also known as a crisis-management operation. Elected officials and city workers failed to see the Sowell problem as a procedural problem; they saw it as a political inconvenience.

What wasn't addressed was the court system that determined Gladys Wade's accusation of assault in December 2008 was not credible while Sowell's explanation was. The coroner's office found that five women—Kim Yvette Smith, Nancy Cobbs, Amelda Hunter, Janice Webb, and Telacia Fortson—died after the Wade case.

It appears that the white-collar law-enforcement workers—prosecutors, judges who might sign warrants, and various paper pushers—are above the fray, while the street cops take the blame.

The state of Ohio has a long way to go in caring for its people, especially those who aren't part of the government superstructure, where pensions and raises are freely handed out despite shoddy performance.

In reading up on the case and talking to people involved, it became apparent to me that there were even more attacks by Sowell that were not reported.

Other families never reported missing loved ones because they were so used to their being missing.

And some reportings are in dispute. Sam Tayeh, who owned the market on Imperial Avenue just feet from the Sowell home, contends families never came to his store with flyers for missing people. Some of the families swear they did. The cops also say that some of the relatives who claim to have reported their loved ones missing never did so. Who is to be believed?

Once the trial was over, I wrote my first letter to Sowell, asking to meet.

My letter began, "Here we are. I am your biographer, and I guess there's not a lot either of us can do about it. I'm a crime writer . . . and you're a convicted criminal. And I am writing your story. I'd like to talk with you, and getting on your visitation list is a good start. We can talk for as much time as they give us, and I'd like to hear it all from you."

It was a pretty straightforward missive, and I didn't want to mislead him with any promises of "equal time" or "fairness." Any report seeks to be fair, but a criminal's idea of fairness is often vastly different than mine.

He responded within a month, asking me to establish an account with Global Tel Link. I did so, and pretty soon, I got a call. The recorded introduction told me I was getting a call from Ohio Correctional Services. I accepted and greeted Sowell.

I was in a car at the time, and he was on speaker. I pulled over to take notes.

Much of what we talked about on that occasion and two others are included in the main story. I confirmed some things and asked more about his jobs, his life growing up in East Cleveland, and his family.

My first goal was to establish some kind of rapport with him, talking sports and geography, since I knew he was pretty good with both. I was following the strategy of defense attorney Rufus Sims, who said Sowell wouldn't communicate with him at first.

Sowell would smile at some of our talk—I could hear it through the phone. He would softly chuckle at a memory. I was again struck by his Southern accent, as out of place as an Irish brogue as far as I was concerned. Where did he get that? Regardless, he seemed to enjoy our chats; we were talking about pleasant things, which is how I wanted it.

My typed notes from one of our conversations:

*One of reasons I got top of my class—to me Marines was the best time of my life I had to come home and helped my mom—*

*I was up for a bonus reenlistment—*

*I came home from Okinawa Japan to camp Pendleton*

*Met Kim in Japan we met—we stayed at round the same rank we were still same rank we split because of me my fault it's a long story—*

*Were moving in next one to three weeks—*

*I had a land line for computer internet use but I used computer at my sisters or library or diff programs I belonged to—I belonged to job programs when first got out I joined this job training program—in Cleveland.*

More notes from another call, these scribbled on the back of a receipt from a repair shop, look like this:

*(heart attack)*

*It affects me really affected me, I couldn't do my job machine operator, coordination was off, everything was off. I was still getting unemployment when I was arrested. It stopped, then I go the extension through the Obama thing, I guess, I found out when I went online to do my taxes with the IRS and it was extended. The VA paid for everything in my heart attack and medicines.*

*Nobody knows about the abuse (in his house as a child)*

*I was a welterweight boxer in the Police Athletic League when I was in high school.*

But these prison calls have a fifteen-minute limit initially. And there's not a lot of room for smoothing things in that short a time frame, then getting to the real questions about living in that house amid the bodies. About Lori and the blame he placed on her for his behavior. About his drug use, which was reported to be prolific. About any other attacks he may have committed.

In February 2012, Sowell sent me a visitor's application for the Death Row Unit at the Chillicothe Correctional Institution. I'm still waiting for it to be approved, even as this book goes to press. If I am, I'll go and report my experience on my website.

I wrote the largest part of this book in a four-hundred-square-foot apartment in Houston, Texas. I was working during the day as an investigative reporter for Texas Watchdog, a news operation bent on transparency and responsibility in government. It was a job that had no end, as you can imagine.

But at night, I would read and reread my notes, pore over transcripts and documents, watch videos of the trial and news reports, check and recheck online court filings, and think about Anthony Sowell. Writing this stuff gets in your head, and sometimes, maybe after reading a particularly disturbing item related to the crime or watching some of the compelling trial testimony, I would take a break and sit on the little porch I had with a view of State Highway 59 and, beyond that, the planes landing at Hobby Airport.

Other times I would sit in silence, studying with the window open as the cars and sirens and planes made their own noise.

I read where the masters, like Steinbeck, and prolific word monsters, like Stephen King, talk of setting word goals for a day or session. Sometimes I would do that, usually around 4,000. Doing a crime book takes more time between sentences in that there are sources that are being tapped, and the facts get in the way of flow. The facts are always getting in the way of something in the eyes of a few. Some even say they get in the way of the story, but you and I know that the best stories are true.

I listened to a lot of music while writing this one, much more than the first two. The soundtrack was a wall of noise at times, German industrial bands like Einstürzende Neubauten or German metal like Rammstein. There was more: Boom Boom Satellites, DJ Shadow, Massive Attack, Test Dept. John Coltrane. One night I blasted through a just-released Tom Waits CD, and I was just paying enough attention to dislike it. It was when I was writing about Tanja Doss, whose hardened testimony gave me big respect for her. Doss's attitude and straight-on, no-bullshit delivery made Waits inconsequential, and I realized—again—that truth always trumps fiction. It's the real deal, something you can hold on to, unlike some sort of artsy phoniness that is supposed to translate into a story. Truth like Tanja's hits you square in the middle of the face.

I was reviewing my notes at one point and noticed that a lot of the trouble for these people, the survivors, started when they were at a bus stop near 140th Avenue and Kinsman. It was there that Anthony Sowell used the ATM for Key Bank.

Bus stop. At any hour. Then I realized that women who were hooking could sit at a bus stop without being hassled by the cops. They could just say they were waiting for a bus. And if it were too late, they could say the time must have escaped them. It was perfect.

These are the things you realize when you sit in a room and think.

On November 12, 2011, I was writing about Shawn Morris, a woman who found herself face-to-face with death in Sowell's house and realized that the only way she was going to survive was to jump out a window on the third floor. She cracked her skull, busted some ribs, and broke both hands. I found myself sad for her and angry at the whole book. It wasn't cathartic to write this in any way.

Reading the transcripts over and over, it was hard to fathom Anthony Sowell killing all these women. Was he evil? Of course, the results were evil. But I really grappled with the idea that he was the devil.

As Larry Sells, the prosecutor in my second true-crime book, *Girl Wanted: The Chase for Sarah Pender*, said of some shady people who were murdered via shotgun at close range, "I don't moralize cases. A lot of the cases I handled didn't have innocent victims, quote unquote. But they didn't deserve to be blown apart by a 12-gauge shotgun and stuffed in a Dumpster like trash. They were druggies and had their problems with the law, but they weren't out killing people."

This is how everyone should feel about the women Sowell killed. Every single one of them had terrible criminal records, some with violent crimes.

To society at large, these were nobody's women. But to their families, these ladies were troubled yet beloved human beings.

We've got a long way to go.